DEDICATED TO MY WIFE LAURIE LEBOWSKY AND MY SUPPORTIVE
CHILDREN JUSTIN AND AMANDA, MY SUPPORTIVE FAMILY LARRY AND
LYNN, AND MY DAD KAL AND IN MEMORY FOR MY MOM SUE FOR
BELIEVING IN ME AND ALLOWING ME TO HELP THOSE IN NEED.

TABLE OF CONTENTS

I started working at a very young age. Being a third-generation retailer and growing up in a family-owned business taught me the value of building relationships and hard work. When business was good, we went to nice places to eat and on elaborate trips. When business was slow, we did smaller trips. That was a simple reality when your family's income was unpredictable. While I learned many things from my parents, the main business lesson I have carried throughout my life is the importance of how you take care of people. I have found that when managing over $700 Million in sales over my career, the engine behind great sales and a profitable business is how you take care of people. Whether it is training, developing, or encouraging people to buy (or give), human interaction and how you build a relationship is paramount to being successful in business. In sales and in human resource management it is the leader's job to find out *what is important* to each individual. If you can figure that out, then you will succeed. If you cannot figure out *what is important* then you lack the urgency or justification for doing business. I have a 30-year track record of excellence in retail store management and corporate training, with 19 of those years of carrying out successful fundraising, strategic planning, and leadership training for a variety of non-profit organizations. If there is one thing that is constant when problems arise, it is the organization's inability to build relationships with their employees and their customers. The more I work for Fortune 250 companies, the less I see consistent efforts in maintaining these relationships.

I continue to devote my energy to organizations and people that are committed to success and growth. By using my education, experience, and ability to lead teams, I want to help corporations and individuals avoid downsizing while improving our US economy. I have developed this book to 1) show corporations how to avoid *downsizing* and improve the relationships they build with their employees and customers, which will not only improve their business performance but also improve our overall US economy, and 2) help those employees who have been *downsized* with tools and resources to build their life and income at or above their expectations.

I think it's helpful to introduce one another so the perspectives of this book and its intentions are clear from the beginning. First, a little bit about me. As I stated in the preface I'm a third-generation retailer. My grandfather moved his retail business from Minnesota to California. His brothers  and sisters joined him in the business. When my dad was old enough he joined his dad in the business. One of my dad's jobs was to travel to small towns and buy closeouts and other merchandise. A closeout is a line of goods that a store cannot sell and they discount it deeply to get rid of it. My dad would go into stores and ask about which sizes or styles were not selling. The owner would collect a pile of clothes for my dad and he would pay in cash for the merchandise, take it back to my grandfather's store and sell it at a high profit. Business was good and my dad provided a lot of leadership and hard work to the business. One day, my dad was reviewing the books and found out he was the lowest-paid employee even though he did most of the work. My grandfather's brothers and sisters made significantly more and did not contribute as much to the business. After arguing with my grandfather, my dad decided to go into business by himself so he found a store directly across the street from my grandfather's business and opened up his store in 1965. Several days later I was born.

At the young age of nine I worked for my dad in his store. It became a well-established clothing store in the heart of

Downsizing by Brad S. Lebowsky

the garment district in Los Angeles, California. I started organizing boxes, sweeping the sidewalk, and cleaning the store. I did not sell my first suit until I was fourteen. I worked with my dad until I was in my mid-twenties. I learned a lot of important lessons regarding building relationships with customers, developing a strong personal connection to employees, and the importance of obtaining the right merchandise at the right price. In addition to all these lessons my dad taught me something very important: have fun when you're working. My dad has a great sense of humor and had fun everyday working in the store. One example I can give you is when my dad would play jokes on his employees. Nothing mean-spirited; my dad wanted to make everyone laugh. My dad's store had a gate near the front door to allow people in. The gate had a loud buzzer to signal everyone in the store when someone was coming through the door. My dad would take a shepherd's hook (a long pole with a hook at the end used to take down merchandise from high above the floor) and gently pull a particular employee's pant leg while someone else rang the door bell. Needless to say this employee jumped up at attention thinking something was getting his leg. The store was in hysterics, including the employee.

My family has a long history of not only retail but service to the community. I knew I had enough retail background to be successful so I wanted to expand my expertise in helping the community. I sought out an MBA program that was specific to nonprofit organizations and I found a great MBA program at the University of Judaism in Los Angeles, California, now called American Jewish University. This MBA program allowed me to grow my professional management style, heighten my level of detail analysis, and sharpen my skills in problem-solving to help community based organizations. After I graduated with honors in 1994 I started my own consulting business. The majority of my practice (85%) is volunteer or pro bono work. Smaller nonprofits need my expertise but cannot afford it so I do what I can to teach them ways to sustain them. I enjoy helping nonprofits seek more funding for their mission and grow their leadership through training and strategic planning. I am passionate about helping people and enjoy doing this work in conjunction with my professional career.

In the late 1980's the garment district became a secondary market compared to the rise of large and elaborate shopping malls. With the combination of lower traffic and closeouts harder to obtain, my dad left the garment district to sell children's clothing. I joined the corporate world of retail at a division of the May Company in 1991. When I interviewed for the job they discounted my retail experience because it was a family business. They started me off in commission sales in the Ralph Lauren department. Determined to prove myself I implemented the sales approach my dad taught me my whole life. My commissions were some of the highest in my department. Several months' later management sat down with me and explained that I would be promoted to children's department supervisor. When I asked why they told me I was making too much money in commissions and wanted to promote me to salary to save money. I did not argue. I began developing my leadership qualities of strong people skills, high level of customer service, and ability to achieve great results quickly. After about six months supervising my department, a recruiter from Bed, Bath, & Beyond contacted me and wanted me to become an assistant manager with their organization. I accepted and started in their West Los Angeles location.

The setup at Bed, Bath, and Beyond did not represent normal retail structure. Their style at the time was to hire as many managers as they could and have them compete with each other to gain a higher manager level at other stores. My location had more than 14 managers working together. When I ran a department I would have three managers under me, most of whom had more experience managing stores. Needless to say it was awkward to navigate around the resentment of other managers. One of my fond memories of Bed, Bath, and Beyond was meeting and helping Whoopi Goldberg. She was one of the nicest celebrities I have ever met. She was kind, soft spoken, and humble of her amazing talent and popularity.

In addition to working at Bed, Bath, and Beyond, the year of 1993 also brought along my first born son, Justin. His birth caused us to relocate to the Pacific Northwest and attempt to provide him a better life at a lower cost. When we moved I had a consulting job lined up since I was finishing my MBA at the time. Unfortunately the business was not legitimate and provided me false financial statements. I pounded the pavement near my rental home in Beaverton, Oregon and walked into Office Depot. The manager there gave me a chance and hired me as a Customer Service Manager (an hourly position). Office Depot gave me the opportunity to grow and learn how to manager larger stores, larger volumes, and more complex transactions. In addition to managing I was one of 14 managers chosen to train commissioned sales associates throughout the country. This was my first official corporate training job and I loved it. In February 1998 I was in my office analyzing some reports and my phone rang. It was a recruiter from Gateway Computers.

I had no idea what a Gateway computer was. After some research and a $12,000 raise, I joined Gateway and helped them open 25 stores in California and Washington. I loved working for Gateway because it was a small operation, lots of sales, great people, great product, and a terrific work-life blend. Why do I say *blend* instead of balance? I don't believe there is an even *balance* between work and family. Most of us work more hours then we see our family especially when multiple members of your family also work. There are 168 hours a week. 56 of those hours are sleeping. 40 to 50 of those hours are working. That leaves 8 hours a day for family. If you take away time to run errands, go to sporting events, etc. there is no even balance of time. Therefore, I emphasize blend where time you do have with family is prioritized and cherished. If Gateway did not close down all their stores I would be working for them today. Their founder Ted Waitt was a great leader and drove the business with a strong commitment to customer service. I really enjoyed his passion and energy around people. I recall when a customer ordered a computer from one of my stores and when the computer arrived it was damaged. It took about a week to build and deliver. My customer needed the computer for a birthday present and we only had a day to get it there. One of the amazing things about Gateway at that time was a manager had access to anyone he or she wanted in order to make a customer happy. I was able to call Ted Waitt's secretary and ask her for help with this computer. I told her it was already in the system but I wanted to ship it next day air to help the customer. She told me to hold on, and I heard her open a door and yell at the production floor *hey…I need this computer built now and shipped today okay?* I was smiling from ear to ear on how cool it was to have this kind of access to our production line and how easy it was to help a customer. The great people in production got the computer assembled and out the door and the very next day UPS delivered it to our customer. Needless to say the customer was thrilled and bragged to all of her friends about the great, prompt service they received from Gateway.

In July of 1998 my daughter Amanda was born as a welcome addition to our family. Three years later, the tech bubble burst in 2001 and we knew that the stores were going to close I began looking for new opportunities. This would be the first time in several years where a recruiter did not call me for another opportunity and I had to find something on my own. While vacationing in California I walked into a Best Buy store and saw one of my mentors from Office Depot, Jeff Fogelman. He bragged about how great Best Buy was and encouraged me to apply. A few interviews later and I was the Assistant Manager at the Spokane Valley location in the State of Washington. I really enjoyed working in this store and in a few short months I was promoted to Store Manager. While all my stories about Best Buy are not very positive, there was a significant amount of time where we had the ability to take care of associates and customers in a way I was comfortable with. I will say more about Best Buy later in the book. For each store I ran, I had the ability to exceed customer expectations and it would reflect on my score card and bonuses. When I had a bonus, over a dozen people on my team got a bonus; it was a good feeling. I had very close teams even though these stores were the largest volume stores in my career. Just as things began to get ugly, Kohl's Department Store recruited me as one of the five managers hired to open up the Portland, Oregon market for the first time. This was an appealing opportunity since I would be opening up a new store from scratch and would not have to go to multiple locations to help *fix* stores and help them perform better.

Kohl's also started out as very customer-focused. Their no-hassle, no-limit return policy was exceptional and a very easy way to build loyalty with customers and employees. We would be allowed to take expired coupons, help with pricing, and encourage customers to take advantage of our many savings throughout any given month. But it was here at Kohl's that I began to be motivated to write this book about **downsizing.** More than in any other company I saw how reduction in hours and elimination of management and full-time positions deeply affect our employees and our customers. Almost 40% of the people that worked for me at my Kohl's location lived in poverty. When their hours were cut or their position eliminated, it was devastating. Most of my employees had multiple jobs and cared for family members and children. This is very difficult to do on part-time hours working slightly above minimum wage. Since most retail jobs attract people without a college education, their ability to find full-time work is extremely challenging. In 2009 our local county had a 14% unemployment rate for those with a high school diploma, 7% for those with a Bachelor's Degree, and 3% for those with a Master's Degree. Not only did I see employees struggle, but our lack of hours and resources affected our customers and their expectation of great service. It was a regular occurrence for me to help support some of my associates in emergency situations which included buying them food, clothes, and one time I bought a used refrigerator for one of my best cashiers because she was hurting and unable to take care of her family. At the wages she was earning in my store, she could not afford a refrigerator large enough to meet her family needs. I did not find that the company understood the impact their decisions could have on people that work and shop in our stores. Once more it was not apparent that they did not try any other methods to improve business or financial results so that they would not have to resort to cutting hours or positions. My recent experience at Kohl's showed me on a small scale what has been happening all over America for a long, long time.

One last thing about me is how I manage people. To know this is to understand better why I approach things the way I do and why I am enthusiastic about helping people. I've set up the 3 P's: **People, Process**, and **Profit**. The most important aspect of my management style is how to engage people. If you can engage people properly then you can teach them the processes they need to be successful. This is done in four key components:

1. **Connections**: The ability to personally connect with my employees and my customer is my first priority as a manager. You cannot begin to lead people without taking the time to get to know them, their families, and to find out *what is important* to them. My strength in building personal relationships has enabled me to not only succeed financially in business but also to create long-lasting relationships. One example

is my friend Mike Dunnel. He was an assistant manager with me at Best Buy. Three years after working together I helped Mike secure a new job at Kohl's. Eight years later I saw Mike in a meeting and we were thrilled to see each other. I recalled his children, his love for flipping houses, and the motorcycle he enjoyed riding. After reminiscing, he told me that the time we had worked together was the best time in his professional life. Most managers are easily forgotten in retail but I strive to create relationships that last a lifetime.

2. **Analytics**: In order to understand your business you have to study all aspects that affect revenue, profit, and growth. While I enjoy analyzing reports and statistical data, I get a majority of my information from people; associates and customers. Feedback is a critical piece of analytics because without it you can miss key information that will help your business grow. At Kohl's I found my conversations with customers to be invaluable. Not only would I learn key perspectives, I was able to correct or improve aspects of my business, where returning customers could see that their feedback was not only heard but implemented. This is a powerful tool when building customer loyalty.

> *...building personal relationships has enabled me to succeed in business.*

3. **Empowerment**: I believe in teaching everyone that works for me not only *how* we need to implement business strategies but *why*. The more employees understand the reasons behind what we must accomplish, the more they own the results. Most retail managers empower only a few and require them to work long hours to accomplish business strategies. It is my philosophy to empower as many people as possible so the work is delegated evenly and more people can share in the success of the team.

4. **Getting Re-elected**: My last management philosophy is a lesson from politics. While I am not a politician, I believe there is an important quality that is required to be re-elected to a trusted office. As a Store Manager, I see myself as a mayor of a small town. Within that town (my store) I am responsible for people's safety, prosperity, and future growth. Unlike most political offices I see myself working towards getting re-elected *daily*. I don't take for granted how hard I need to work to help people and promote my company's strategic initiatives. If I put in the time, the care, and the effort, I am able to be re-elected so that I can manage and lead for another day.

Now that you know a little about me, let us talk about you.

 For those of you who manage in corporate America, I would like you to see this book as well-documented evidence that *downsizing* is one of the few corporate strategies implemented with little thought and little financial success over time. That sentence will cause you to pause because corporations are often rewarded by Wall Street when they save money or produce higher profits by *downsizing*. But what Wall Street cannot see is the day-to-day operations, loss of market share, and the difficulty in maintaining strong financial performance (savings) over time. Oftentimes we find that *downsizing* is a quick, last-chance strategy designed as a quick result for a troubling time or downturn in business. The great thing about corporate America reading this book is that you will get a perspective from evidence-based research on how *downsizing* is the least effective tool for improving financial performance. All levels of managers will be able to understand the history and financial landscape of *downsizing* and incorporate some of the ideas in this book to avoid *downsizing* and help your company realize a stronger and longer lasting financial performance. While there will be many levels of management from corporate American reading this book, there is a focus on CEO influence on the financial performance and expense control of a corporation. Later in the book I will show you economic evidence that CEO pay has been on the rise as much as 40% where *middle class* wages have remained flat since the 1990's. Try not to be defensive on this issue.

CEO's are amassing wealth, which is causing economic class inequality and negatively affecting Wall Street, your stock value, and the amount of consumer spending in the US economy. Not unlike any other expense in your business, it is important to see CEO pay as a portion of your overall payroll expense structure. If another area of your business had a higher than average expense it would cause attention.

One of my goals in this book is to have you consider alternatives to CEO pay that outpace the norm and your average worker. To drastically cut one expense, and drastically increase another expense, is not the standard or recommended business practice. You will see research that proves that *downsizing* wreaks havoc on the US economy, which affects your pocketbook and those of your children and grandchildren. If you could discover a way to help your business, improve the US economy, and stabilize your family, then you would probably entertain a new way of thinking. This book will provide you many options to consider instead of *downsizing* to improve your business, grow your business, and sustain your local town, city, and state. But why should corporate American care about the communities around them? It's simple, because they are your customers. Consumer spending can make up 70% of the country's GDP and continues to have significant impact on unemployment and the economy in general. You will find in this book that when consumer spending is down, it sends Wall Street down and when that happens your stocks are devalued. That negative trend affects all publically traded corporations. This is a proven cycle:

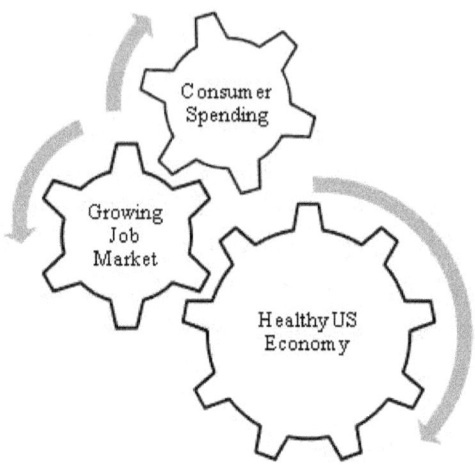

How corporations look at this cycle and how they invest their profits is critical to every man, woman, and child in the United States. Regardless of size, every business contributes to the US economy, their neighbors, and the world. If corporations continue to eliminate jobs, increase their profits, and not circulate the profits back into the US economy, recessions can reoccur and stock market crashes will be constant. I realize that CEO's are skeptical about investing their profits in the larger public. Such an action in today's climate can be viewed as irresponsible and reckless. Let us use a house located in a residential neighborhood as an example.

Imagine your house among other similar homes in the same neighborhood. If you maintain your house with fresh paint, a well-maintained yard, and a property clear of debris, you will add value not only to your house but to the entire neighborhood. When you add improvements on the inside of your house that include higher end counter tops, technological advances such as home theater system, and energy efficient improvements to save money you will add value to your house. When you sell your home, these values not only affect your asking price but the value of every home in your block. This is an analogy of what could happen if corporations and their CEO's invest in their own business **and** the community around them. Let us look at the opposite reaction. Imagine if you were a homeowner who did not take care of your yard. The paint on your house was peeling and you have debris throughout your front and back yard. You are basically saving money by not taking care of your property or making improvements. When your neighbor tries to sell their house, buyers will take into account your horrible-looking property, and that will bring down the value of your neighbor's house. When your neighbor complains you simply say *I don't care, I'm saving my money and I don't care what happens to you.* As some senior managers and CEO's can live in high-end communities, one can imagine that their high income-earning neighbors would not tolerate such neglect of their property. This analogy applies to the current climate of corporations. We will continue to illustrate many examples of growing companies that *downsize* the middle class and reward their CEO's for doing so, never realizing true long term improved financial performance for their company.

In this book I will prove to CEO's and large corporations throughout the US that investing profits in growing the economy will grow your business at a higher rate than you currently experience. While profits can help increase the value of corporate stock, a downward economy can send stocks falling regardless of a company's business performance. Corporate America will find in the examples and proven evidence in this book that an investment in people yields a more stable, higher-growth stock performance over time. I want corporate America to look at this book and realize the proven alternatives to *downsizing* so they can realize a greater corporate image, a consistent flow of profits, and a stabilized business that will continue to grow using their greatest resource to fuel growth: **people.**

GREETINGS EVERY DAY WORKERS

The reason why I want you to read this book is to better understand how corporations work and the pressure that exists for them to improve profits year over year. Similar to  how you look at your family, businesses want to be stable and grow over time. They want to provide themselves with upgraded equipment, powerful marketing tools, and the ability to realize their true potential. Every day workers are weary of those corporations that find *downsizing* as a regular tool for cutting costs. Most workers come to work wanting to contribute and help their company succeed. But at times, workers are not part of the thought process behind strategies that will help a failing business improve. It is important for you to read this book so that you can develop ideas for how you can be part of the problem-solving process. In addition, if you are a product of *downsizing*, I have tools and ideas to help you find a new job and stabilize yourself and your family. These strategies, while sometimes hard to realize, are extremely effective in recovering from a loss of hours or a job loss. As I want corporations to start investing in people and our US economy, I want everyday workers to think about their role in the US economy and how important it is to have an income that will support a comfortable and safe lifestyle while providing children with a higher education and a hope for greater stability in their lives. Everything you invest in yourself, your company, and your community will be directly related to how your life will be in the future (e.g. retirement). And if you have children, everything you do will affect how they create their success and the level of difficulty in realizing their potential and providing for their families. In addition to your effort, everyday workers must invest in training or a higher education throughout their work life. The more you can learn about innovations, future trends, and stronger skills the more stable your employment will be. From books to seminars, college to trade schools, everyday workers must continue to grow their knowledge, because as I show later in this book, you can realize a higher wage with higher learning.

> *...people who work together will win, whether it be against complex football defenses, or the problems of modern society.* **Vince Lombardi**

Another important goal of this book is to have the everyday worker understand economic history and how it has shaped the workforce today. It is important to understand how Wall Street and corporate profits influence the political process and financial policies that affect your pay, your work, and your overall stability. Many different aspects will be presented through established researchers and experts in the field. Facts and opinions are necessary to understand the true picture of what has happened, what is currently happening, and what may happen in the future. Understanding these facts will help you and your family navigate through a very difficult time.

For all people, corporations, and the future of our children, we must work together toward a common goal that includes everyone in the winning outcome. Profits cannot be used for CEO's alone; they must be shared for managers, employees, and communities in order to stabilize our US economy and provide more opportunities for all levels of income. As Henry Ford said: *Coming together is a beginning; keeping together is progress; working together is success.* Vince Lombardi adds "*People who work together will win, whether it be against complex football defenses, or the problems of modern society.*" It is my sincere hope and passion that this book produces great success where corporations, employees and communities can all profit from one another while growing our US economy.

Downsizing by corporations or nonprofit organizations can take many forms. For most, the term *downsizing* suggests layoffs or reduction in staff that has resulted in millions of jobs over the decades. *Downsizing* can also be reduction in hours, pay raise freezes, reduction in pay, and reclassification of jobs, restructuring of staff which may include removal of seasoned employees or reducing full time head count, and limiting the staffing levels of various cost centers. *Downsizing* exists because companies know their largest controllable expense is *payroll*. When things go wrong, become unprofitable, or sales projections go into the negative, corporations can resort to a fast and easy approach of cutting costs; *downsizing*. Corporations have tried to persuade us that these fast cost cutting measures will turn around financial performance. Wall Street experts often applaud corporations for taking swift action to turn around financial performance but are they looking at the long term results of downsizing to determine if the company is actually performing better? This book will explore this myth and unveil the truths about *downsizing* and how corporations can avoid it.

To give you an idea of what *downsizing* may look like in the retail world let's talk about Macy's. During the 2008 recession Macy's needed drastic cost cutting measures. In 2009 Macy's would eliminate 7,000 jobs which included 40.0% of the executive positions.[1] This includes 11 stores closures in nine states. This would help them realize a $400 million savings.[2] What Macy's did is take several salaried managers and make them hourly associates. Many supervisor positions were eliminated while others had to re-apply for their jobs. Managers saw their salaries substantially decreased and many seasoned supervisors lost their jobs not because they were not performing but because they were too expensive and Macy's needed to save money. As Macy's made other business changes and started winning customers back they did not increase their hiring or change their management structure. There are some stores in the Macy's chain that have only one salaried manager; the store manager. This is typical in retail to maintain the same level of workload (sometimes a greater workload) and reduce the number of staff and leaders to manage the workload. Customer demands remain high and those remaining have to increase their productivity and take on more responsibility to make their jobs successful. Some retailers do this very well and implement careful planning to ensure the employees can be successful. Other retailers just keep asking for more and fail to create structure for the employees to accomplish the goals.

Another example of *downsizing* is perhaps one of the largest in history. In 1993, IBM eliminated over 60,000 jobs. This was their first major layoff in the company's 79 year history. The Los Angeles Times reported that *IBM announced an $8-billion second-quarter loss and the elimination of 35,000 more jobs by the end of 1994.*[3] Part of the financial downturn was due to the declining market for main frames computers. When the massive layoffs occurred, IBM's new chairman, Louis V. Gerstner Jr. was quoted to say *The last thing IBM needs right now is a vision.*[4] When large corporations have substantial losses due to their business model they will often turn to ***downsizing*** to show immediate and drastic cuts to prove to Wall Street they are being *fiscally responsible*. As you will learn in this book, ***downsizing*** has little correlation to a real improved financial performance. But because IBM provided Wall Street with what they wanted, their shares increased $3.25 a share even though they posted a multi-<u>Billion</u> dollar loss. So Wall Street rewarded the company for failing and punished 60,000 workers who had little or nothing to do with IBM's business problems. IBM rewarded Gerstner with an $8.5 Million potential income for *fixing* the companies problems.

While most Americans have experienced ***downsizing*** in one form or another, it's important to understand the historical perspective on how we got to this point in our economy. It's well known that understanding the past can prevent problems for our future. Confucius said: *Study the past if you would define the future.*

HISTORICAL PERSPECTIVE

Downsizing has been used as a cost cutting tool for corporations for decades. The *New York Times* article, *The Downsizing of America* stated that more than 43 million jobs were lost in the United States since 1979, affecting nearly one-third of all households.[5] The other two-thirds of households are affected by negative effects of ***downsizing*** due to the unstable US economy, higher interest rates, and lower consumer spending. More than 85 percent of the Fortune 500 firms have experienced at least one episode of downsizing by 1994.[6] Since the 1980's, large organizations and corporations believed that reducing staff would increase efficiency. In order to truly understand *downsizing* we must examine its origin, the companies that took advantage of it and the sustainable results (if any) from reducing staff. Critical research by E. Geoffrey Love and Nitin Nohria[7] documented Fortune 100 firms from 1978 to 1999 which eliminated over five million employees.[8] The American Management Association conducted a study that a quarter of the companies it studied had at least *three* episodes of *downsizing*.[9] This suggests that *downsizing* did not work the first time or the corporation did not improve financially so they tried *downsizing* again, then again. Most businesses would not repeat strategies that fail once let alone twice but *downsizing* is typically repeated because while it may not improve financial performance it does save money immediately. Let's use *New Coke* as an example. In 1985, the Coca-Cola Company decided to rebrand their classic and well known Coke brand and change it to *New Coke*. This idea was a failure and Coca-Cola had *to re-launch its original brand and called it Classic Coke for the US market.*[10] As you can imagine Coca-Cola lost Millions of dollars in this failed ad campaign. What are the odds they would repeat the same mistake and try to remarket *New Coke* in 2014? In some cases when companies gained savings from *downsizing* it has gone to CEO pay which I'll talk about later in the book.

In 2001 many companies *downsized* due to a recession that was caused by the tech bubble bursting and September 11th which created substantial job loss. In addition the scandals of Enron, WorldCom, and Tyco cost many people their jobs and their retirement savings. One example includes the Dow Chemical company that would eliminate $1.1

billion in costs including 4,500 jobs, as the result of an economic slowdown.[11] In the first four months of 2001, **572,370 job cuts** were announced.[12]

JOB LOSS VERSUS UNEMPLOYMENT

While unemployment occurs as a result of *downsizing,* we must also consider jobs that are eliminated or *lost* which speaks to instability. *Job loss* is defined as the *disappearance of jobs because of fundamental structural economic changes as distinct from transient fluctuations in demand.*[13] Unemployment is defined as *a person who is actively searching for employment is unable to find work.*[14] While low unemployment rates occurred during this time period, job *loss* rates increased. For example in the two years from 1981 to 1983, the job *loss* rate was 3.5 percentage points **higher** than the *unemployment* rate; by the 2001–2003 period, that difference had grown to **7 percent higher.**[15] From 2000 to 2003 the manufacturing sector of the US economy *lost* **2.85 million jobs** as a result of trade and the downturn in the economy; one example of a fundamental structural change.[16] People were not *downsized* but jobs that would have been filled by US workers were shipped overseas therefore *lost.*

The 2008 recession was caused by several market failures which resulted in businesses closing and *downsizing* activities to be the highest in our country's history. Most are aware of the housing markets and financial markets collapsing due to high risk investments and questionable mortgage loans. During this time the Bureau of Labor statistics showed 6.9 million persons with at least 3 years of tenure at their company were eliminated.[17] In 2011 the Hamilton Project analyzed job *loss* from this recession and that between *October of 2008 and April of 2009, an average of 700,000 American workers lost their jobs each month — contributing to the worst sustained decline in employment since the Great Depression.*[18]

Over 25 million American workers are now unemployed or underemployed which is twice as many Americans out of work in 1933 (The Great Depression).[19] For the hopes of all businesses that **downsized** from 2008 to 2010, improved financial performance was the justification for massive reductions of human capital. A significant amount of research shows that financial performance was not consistently gained by these reductions which I'll show you later in this book.

Important Points:

- *Downsizing* exists because companies know their largest controllable expense is payroll.
- *Downsizing* has little correlation to long term improved financial performance.
- More than 85 percent of the Fortune 500 firms have experienced at least one episode of downsizing.
- Over 25 million American workers are now unemployed or underemployed.

CONSUMER SPENDING

When you analyze the history of *downsizing* you must also analyze the economy of the United States. Economists (not just politicians) have stated that the *middle class* or working class is the fuel for the US economy. The economy can be measured in thousands of different ways. One way is through consumer spending. During the decade from 1990s to 2000, consumer spending on goods and services in the US **increased 3.3** percent per year where the employment generated from this spending grew at **1.8 percent** per year.[20] The unemployment rate in 1990 was 5.6% ending in 2000 at 4%.[21] This illustrates a stronger economy prior to the job loss during the 2001 recession discussed earlier. So long as the *middle class* had money to spend on housing, food, and services, the economy grew jobs. During this time employment generated by consumer spending was 83.2 million total workers, accounting for **62 percent** of total employment in the economy.[22] It is simple to conclude that without consumer spending, our economy would be in shambles. In fact if it was not for the **62 percent** or the *middle class*, our top tier income achievers would be considerably devalued.

One example is Donald Trump, known for premier properties and hotels. While most people in the top income brackets can afford these properties it's the **62 percent** of the workers who create the top income levels through their spending. If consumer spending declines as fast as unemployment grows, Mr. Trump's clients would lose wealth dramatically and not be able to afford his premier properties. If that happens, Mr. Trump ends up with properties that are vacant and therefore not generating income and if that persists, Mr. Trump himself could lose a substantial amount of wealth. Many economists agree that consumers must buy goods and services to create a growing US economy. While exporting is a portion of what makes the US economy work, consumer spending is a key factor in sustaining positive growth. In 2003, U.S. consumer spending accounted for around 70 percent of U.S. gross domestic product (GDP).[23]

I have worked in the retail environment for over 30 years. Our industry is known to measure a portion of consumer spending as a way to analyze the health of the economy. In 2011, the amount spent on retail goods in the US was $3.8 trillion.[24] For this sector, the holiday season (November and December) can represent 20% to 40% of annual sales depending on the corporation.[25] Retail corporations consistently *downsize* many times throughout the year including reduction in hours, layoffs, and management changes. I believe that all companies that *downsize* reduce consumer spending in the retail sector. For retailers, their employees can be their best customers. When retailers *downsize*, they eliminate customers and reduce sales which negatively affect our economy.

The *tech* bubble from 2000 to 2001 and the terrorist attacks on September 11th caused a temporary recession negatively affecting the US economy. During this time period consumer spending continued to grow in small amounts. No decline in consumer spending was reported until the recession of 2008.[26] The unemployment rate in 2001 was 4.7% and reached a peak of 6.0% in 2003.[27] As you can see, even in the event of a recession, jobs are still growing but at a much lower rate than before. The job rate affected the growth in consumer spending. Before the 2001 recession consumer spending grew quarter after quarter starting in 1997 at 1.1% in the first quarter, 1.7% in the third quarter and 1.2% in the fourth quarter.[28] When the effects of the recession started in 2001, consumer spending growth fell below 1% at 0.3% in the first quarter of 2002 and staying below 1% until the second quarter of 2003 at 1.1%.[29] The decrease of jobs directly correlates to the decrease in consumer spending. As consumer spending fell during the 2001 recession *downsizing* was in full swing; responding to the negative economy. It was understood by major corporations that if they cut expenses, mostly payroll, they would survive the recession. By eliminating jobs the corporations extended the recession and made the US economy, as well as their own financial performance, weaken. As soon as they started adding jobs after 2003, consumer spending increased and the US economy stabilized. This is just one of many examples that show a direct relationship between *downsizing*, consumer spending, and the US economy.

The 2008 recession was the worst recession in my lifetime. Over 7 Million jobs were lost from 2007 in the US economy.[30] To provide you an historical perspective it took the US economy 39 months after 2001 to regain lost jobs. According to authors James Manyika and Susan Lund it may take more than *60 months to recover from the 2008 recession*.[31] The unemployment rate for 2008 was 5.8% and in one year grew to 9.3%.[32] Kevin Lansing, an economist at the Federal Reserve Bank of San Francisco notes that *42 months past the start of the 2008 recession, consumer expenditures are still **1.6 percent** below their pre-recession peak*.[33] When consumer

> *...corporate profits stood at 14.2 percent in the third quarter of 2012, the largest share at any time since 1950, while the portion of income that went to employees was 61.7 percent, near its lowest point since 1966.*

spending shrinks it affects every major business and household in the US. Everyone watching a television set could see the affects of people affected by the decrease in consumer spending and the hurt it put on the US economy. Many businesses suffered losses and employees that lost their jobs lost their homes, and significant wealth. Health concerns as a result of the economy became abundant and serious.

WALL STREET

In addition to consumer spending, Wall Street is a barometer to investors that also makes the US economy work. Let's learn a little bit about how Wall Street acts and how Wall Street can influence business. First there are two types of markets; a **Bull** which is known as symbol of aggressive financial optimism.[34] When businesses profit, investors want a piece of the profits so they buy and sell stocks and collect their reward. A **Bear** market has historically occurred when there is a sharp fall in the market, a strong rally in prices for several months, which may lull some investors into thinking that the bear market is over, and a downward fall in prices as share valuations reach rock bottom.[35] Wall Street investors, and there are millions of them, watch profits closely to determine if they believe a company will succeed or fail. This seems obvious but what is hidden behind the veil is the lack of understanding of how the profit is realized. Corporations have to portray their financial performance honestly but what they don't have to do is go into finite detail of how they became more profitable. Wall Street may look at the bottom line, reads a few blurbs on what the company is dreaming about, then decide to invest or sell shares in that company. Wall Street also focuses on political activity, the Federal Reserve, and other economic trends to help them calculate their investment strategies. For the purpose of this book we're going to focus on a company's profit.

When a company reports big profits or profits that exceed their estimated expectations their stock price rises. This is pretty common. Here is a similar phrase you can read often about profit and stock prices from the Los Angeles Times stating **Bulls** *hope that stronger corporate profits will help the underlying value of stocks and keep this year's rally going.*[36] You will seldom see stock prices go down when companies are profitable unless there is something going on in Congress or a government shutdown is looming. In comparison here is a typical warning from CBS Money Watch: *Warnings of weaker sales sent the stock market spiraling lower as Wal-Mart cut its estimates for annual revenue and profit, warning that cautious shoppers are spending less.*[37] When President Obama took office in 2008 the Dow Industrial Average was floating around 7,000 points. After job recovery took place and corporations **downsized** the market is floating around 15,000 points in September 2013. So if corporations are experiencing higher profits which drive up stock prices thereby driving up the Dow Industrial Average, then why are so many people unemployed? The New York Times writes *as a percentage of national income, corporate profits stood at 14.2 percent in the third quarter of 2012, the largest share at any time since 1950, while the portion of income that went to employees was 61.7 percent, near its lowest point since 1966.*[38] Why would companies not invest their profits by hiring more people thus growing the US economy? It's simple; Wall Street investors don't reward them for hiring people. The reward is showing higher profits. We spoke earlier how consumer spending can be as much as 70% of our GDP and a major catalyst for our US economy. So keeping people unemployed shrinks consumer spending and puts a strain on the US economy, a strain that can ultimately affect the corporations who are perpetuating this problem.

In terms of Wall Street terms another familiar term is a *bubble.* This is how recessions have been described as the "tech *bubble*" in 2001 or the "housing *bubble*" in 2008. The market has bubbles continuously and when the Dow industrial average reaches above 11,000 points it creates a bubble that fluctuates over various market reactions. While writing this book, the market has exceeded 16,000 points; a delicate *bubble* that must be considered and class inequality can be an economic force that can burst that *bubble.*

ECONOMIC CLASS INEQUALITY

Donald Trump exemplifies the 1% of our country that is the highest income earners. This is a significant point in understanding our US economy, consumer spending, and the *middle class.* As we've discussed since the 1980's, our US economy has moved through **downsizing** and recessions. In the 1980's there were three easily visible classes in the United States. In an article entitled *Wealth, Income, and Power* by G. William Domhoff from the University of California at Santa Cruz, has some helpful charts below to show how wealth has shifted economic classes over the years.

Table 1: Income, net worth, and financial worth in the U.S. by percentile, in 2010 dollars[39]

Wealth or income class	Mean household income	Mean household net worth	Mean household financial (non-home) wealth
Top 1 percent	$1,318,200	$16,439,400	$15,171,600
Top 20 percent	$226,200	$2,061,600	$1,719,800
60th-80th percentile	$72,000	$216,900	$100,700
40th-60th percentile	$41,700	$61,000	$12,200
Bottom 40 percent	$17,300	-$10,600	-$14,800

From Wolff (2012); only mean figures are available, not medians. Note that income and wealth are separate measures; so, for example, the top 1% of income-earners is not exactly the same group of people as the top 1% of wealth-holders, although there is considerable overlap.[40]

Table 2: Distribution of net worth and financial wealth in the United States, 1983-2010[41]

	Total Net Worth		
	Top 1 percent	Next 19 percent	Bottom 80 percent
1983	33.8%	47.5%	18.7%
1989	37.4%	46.2%	16.5%
1992	37.2%	46.6%	16.2%
1995	38.5%	45.4%	16.1%
1998	38.1%	45.3%	16.6%
2001	33.4%	51.0%	15.6%
2004	34.3%	50.3%	15.3%
2007	34.6%	50.5%	15.0%
2010	35.4%	53.5%	11.1%

This chart allows us to see from 1983 to 2010 how wealth has evaporated from the bottom 80%. In 1983 the 19% or upper/middle class had most of the wealth in the United States. The difference between the 19% and the top 1% was about 14% where the difference between the upper/middle class the rest of us was 29%. In 2010 the difference between the upper/middle class and the rest of us was 42%; a **45% decrease in wealth to 80% of the US population**.

Another article in Mother Jones entitled *It's the Inequality, Stupid* by Dave Gilson and Carolyn Perot states *the top one-hundredth of one percent, who now make an average of $27 million per household.*[42] One chart in this article shows who is winning and who is losing in our current US economy.

GAINS AND LOSSES, 2007-2009

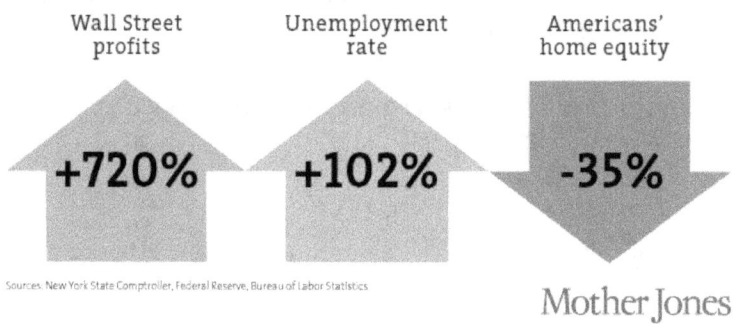

Wall Street profits   Unemployment rate   Americans' home equity

+720%   +102%   -35%

Sources: New York State Comptroller, Federal Reserve, Bureau of Labor Statistics

Mother Jones

43

CNBC reported on August 22nd 2012 that *a study from Pew Research finds that middle-income Americans have seen their median net worth **remain roughly flat** over the past **quarter-century**, at $93,150 in 2010, compared to $91,056 in 1983.*[44] The article goes on to describe the opposite trend for the upper income families that *have seen their median net worth grow over the same period by 87 percent, to $574,788 from $307,134.*[45]

It has been reported by David DeGraw that since the 2008 financial crisis, *the top one percent and the remaining 99% of the US population has grown to a record high where the top one percent owns over 70% of all financial assets, an all time record.*[46] In 2010 Rick Newman with US News and World Report analyzed data from Heidi Shierholz of the Economic Policy Institute and the Census Bureau to break down household income into nine brackets. Rick Newman found that *to represent the middle class, with income ranging from $35,000 to $99,999, shows that households account for 43.7 percent of all households compared to 2000 at 45.6 percent, 1990 at 47.9 percent, and 1980 at 49.3 percent.*[47]

There is a substantial amount of evidence that our *middle class* is shrinking in the US economy; only the upper income families are growing in wealth. Another source of data for economic classes comes from the Congressional Budget Office (CBO) which is a nonpartisan, independent analysis of budgetary and economic issues in the United States.[48] In 2010 the CBO shows that in 2007, *the average household in the top 1 percent had an income of $1.3 million, up $88,800 just from the prior year; this $88,800 gain is well above the total 2007 income of the average middle-income household ($55,300).*[49] This chart shows a dramatic image:

...middle-income Americans have seen their median net worth remain roughly flat over the past quarter-century.

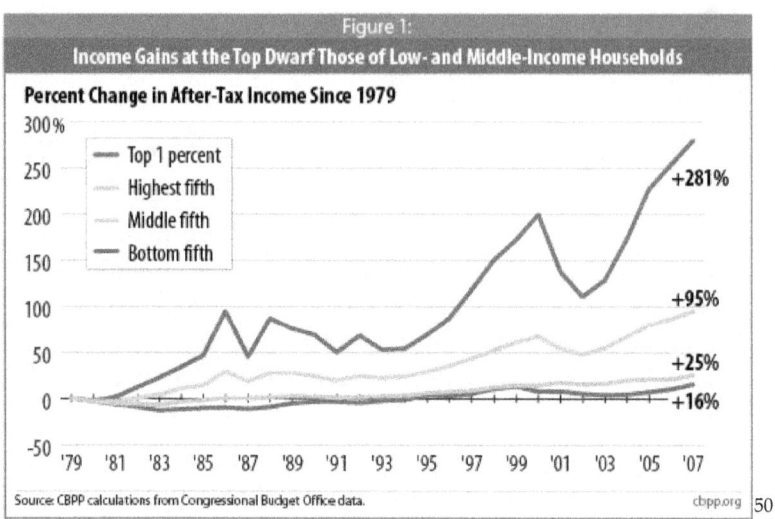

Figure 1:
Income Gains at the Top Dwarf Those of Low- and Middle-Income Households

Percent Change in After-Tax Income Since 1979

- Top 1 percent
- Highest fifth
- Middle fifth
- Bottom fifth

+281%
+95%
+25%
+16%

Source: CBPP calculations from Congressional Budget Office data.   cbpp.org 50

While it is easy to see how the upper income families are growing in wealth at a higher rate than any other class, it may not be easy to figure out in which class your family belongs. While there is much discussion about what people think and about what the Census Bureau deems *middle class*, the one easy way to determine your economic class is look at your bank account. If you are making more money than you did 10 years ago, congratulations, you're showing mobility in our economic class system. For most of us who do not see any growth in income, we're hanging around the middle to lower classes. Your bank account is directly proportional to your ability to spend. But why is understanding these economic classes important to understanding the economy?

In a New York Times article quoting President Obama as saying *when middle-class families have less to spend, guess what? Businesses have fewer consumers. When wealth concentrates at the very top, it can inflate unstable bubbles that threaten the economy.*[51] This is one type of *bubble* I was referring to the previous section. This is a good summary of what we've discussed thus far. A lack of mobility and inequality of economic class threatens our economy just as much as high risk mortgage loans. Our tax code is another factor that creates inequality in middle to lower classes. Comparisons by Richard Wolff of the Guardian illustrates taxes *at the end of the second world war, for every dollar Washington raised in taxes on individuals, it raised $1.50 in taxes on business profits. Today* (in 2011), *for every dollar Washington gets in taxes on individuals, it takes* **25 cents** *in taxes on business which puts the burden of federal taxation off business and* **onto individuals**.[52] While people will argue that taxing businesses takes money away from job creation, Mr. Wolff observes that *even with low taxes on businesses and the rich, money is not being invested into creating jobs. It is not being distributed to anyone else and so is not being spent on consumer goods either.*[53] Through CEO pay and businesses realizing larger than ever profits kept for them only is another way class inequality has grown in the US. In the last five years, these profits have been used to fuel political campaigns and legislation to help businesses get more breaks and incentives while the middle and lower classes have not benefited from corporations rise in profits.

With the Supreme Court passing *Citizens United* which gave Corporations legal standings to donate unlimited resources to Political campaigns without any disclosure has caused more class inequality due to the influence this money can bring. Robert Reich from the University of California, Berkeley believes that *with hefty campaign*

> ...the nation's biggest disparities, from education and life expectancy to poverty, are increasingly due to economic class position.

*contributions and platoons of lobbyists and public relations
spinners, America's executive class has gained lower tax rates
while resisting reforms that would spread the gains from growth.*[54]

Occupy Wall Street started as a response to rising income
inequality. Their recently published mission statement
includes that *no true democracy is attainable when the process
is determined by economic power,* to oppose *bailouts from
taxpayers while Executives enjoy exorbitant bonuses* and
*outsourced labor and used that outsourcing as leverage to cut
workers' healthcare and pay.*[55] This graphic from Occupy
Wall Street is a dramatic example of what they peacefully
stand for:

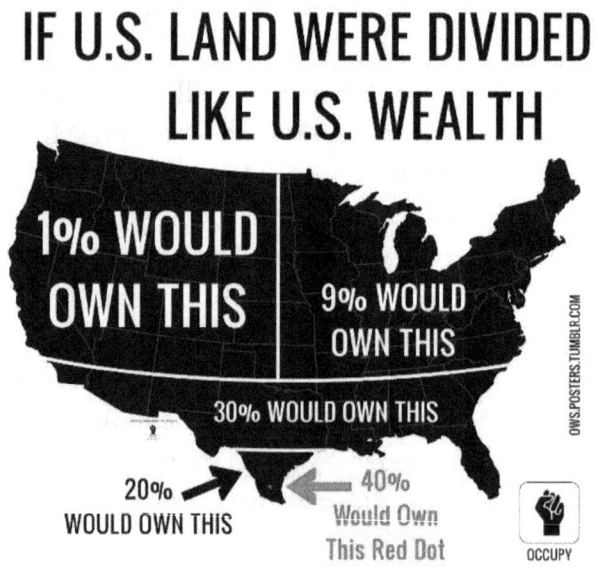

Harvard Professor William Julius Wilson states, *it's time that America comes to understand that many of the nation's biggest disparities, from education and life expectancy to poverty, are increasingly due to* **economic class position.**[56] So how does this affect you corporate America? How does this affect you the average worker? A survey by the Associated Press believes that by *2030, close to 85 percent of all working-age adults in the U.S. will experience bouts of economic insecurity.*[57] [58] The definition for economic security and the *middle class* can be one and the same. The U. S. Department Of Commerce Economics and Statistics Administration in January 2010 states that *middle class families are defined by their aspirations more than their income* which include *home ownership, a car, college education for their children, health and retirement security and occasional family vacations.*[59] These aspirations mirror average consumer spending patterns. This report also shows us how pricing throughout the years has increased making it more difficult for US families to maintain *middle class* status.

We've already proven *middle class* incomes have remained flat and now with prices increasing create more inequality and push the *middle class* closer to the lower classes.

Table 5

Price Changes in Key Middle Class Items: 1990 - 2008

	Actual 1990 prices	Actual 2008 prices	Actual price changes	Inflation Adjustment		
				1990 prices in 2008 dollars	Actual 2008 prices	Price changes in inflation-adjusted terms*
Housing *(Median value)*	$79,100	$197,600	150%	$126,600	$197,600	56%
Health Care *(Premiums and out-of-pocket expenses)*	$1,200	$5,100	325%	$2,000	$5,100	155%
College						
Four-year public college *(Tuition, fees, and room and board)*	$5,200	$13,400	158%	$8,400	$13,400	60%
Four-year private college *(Tuition, fees, and room and board)*	$13,200	$30,400	130%	$21,200	$30,400	43%

* One way to interpret this column is to recognize that it shows price changes in excess of economy-wide inflation.

Sources:

Housing: U.S. Census Bureau, 2008 American Community Survey (Table B25077) and 1990 Decennial Census (Table H023B).

Health Care Expenses: Bernard D., Banthin J. Family Level Expenditures on Health Care and Insurance Premiums among the Nonelderly Population, 2006. Research Findings No. 29. March 2009. Agency for Healthcare Research and Quality, Rockville, MD. Gabel, Jon R., Paul B. Ginsburg, Jeremy D. Pickreign, and James D. Reschovsky "Trends In Out-Of-Pocket Spending By Insured American Workers, 1990-1997." Health Affairs. March/April 2001.

College: U.S. Department of Education, National Center for Education Statistics. (2009). Digest of Education Statistics, 2008 (NCES 2009-020), Table 331.

Note: While we calculated the 1990 and 2008 prices for housing, health care and college using actual information on their cost, there are also published price indexes for housing, medical care, and college. Consistent with this table, all of these indexes also show substantially higher price increases in these commodities than is shown in the aggregate CPI.

(Chart reference[60])

This is yet another example where businesses are making more profit by charging *middle class* families more for goods and services. At the same time businesses **downsize** and reduce the workforce causing financial instability and unemployment. In this scenario *middle class* families earn less yet have to **pay more** for services. How much did profits increase for these businesses? Let's take a look at Healthcare to find out. As we can see on the chart above price changes in Healthcare from 1990 have increased 325%. When you calculate profit dollars you first have to look at Total GDP. In 1990 the US GDP was $5.75 Trillion. The portion of GDP spent on healthcare was 12.2%.[61] This equals $701 billion spent and when you multiply this number by the 14% profit margin realized in 1990[62] it equals $98 billion in profit. Now let's look at 2010 metrics regarding healthcare. The total GDP in 2010 was $14 Trillion. The portion of GDP spent on Health Care was 17.8%.[63] This equals $2.6 Trillion spent and when you multiply that by the 9.3% profit margin for healthcare[64] equals $238 Billion. That is an increase of **$140 billion**. This money has not been invested in lowering rates or expanding coverage. While some of this profit could be invested in research, a portion of this profit has stayed with the company and their CEOs.

Another term for inequality in economic status is *class war*. Susan Milligan with US News World and Report characterizes a *class war* as *the arrogance of executives who believe they should be rewarded just for being executives, forcing workers and consumers and taxpayers to pay when their business venture went south.*[65] Part of the problem that creates **downsizing** and economic collapse is where CEO's of corporations put profits over people. But how do you fix this problem? How do you increase mobility among economic classes? Later in this book we'll discuss some ideas.

Corporations want you to believe they are participating in social responsibility by putting out healthier foods and energy efficient cars. This myth is busted when you examine the higher profits realized by such endeavors. The Wall Street Journal reported in 2010 that *the movement for corporate social responsibility is in direct opposition to the movement for better corporate governance, which demands that managers fulfill their fiduciary duty to act in the shareholders' interest or be relieved of their responsibilities.*[66] The fiduciary duty is normally solely related to rise in profits quarter after quarter, year after year. Re-directing profits to altruistic efforts such as job creation, job relocation (which we'll talk about later), and job training may be career suicide for some CEOs. Harvard Business School Professor Michael Porter wrote that *businesses must reconnect company success with social progress, a new way to achieve economic success.*[67] This *shared value* theory argues that companies should address society's problems by developing new business opportunities and create a source of new profits.[68] In 2009 the Bank of Finland looked at companies that were included or excluded in a key social responsibility ranking and *the study found that stocks dropped an average 3 percent when a company was removed from a list of socially responsible companies.*[69] This may not be proof enough for Wall Street and skeptical CEO's. Could a CEO make a case that job creation and more social responsibility can increase profits and make Wall Street happy? Let's do some math!

The total size of publically traded companies in the US (those that trade on Wall Street) is referred to as *market capitalization*; the share price times the number of shares outstanding for domestic (US) companies. The *market capitalization* does not include investment companies, mutual funds, or other collective investment vehicles.[70] The total *market capitalization* in the US for 2013 was $18,668,333,210,000. Now let's assume that on average these stocks may gain (profit) 4% as an arbitrary easy to use number. That would equal $746,733,328,400 in profits. Now let's take 1% of their total profit which would equal $7,467,333,284. What if we take their 1% of profits and invest it in job creation? For simplicity purposes let's hire people making an average of $45,000 a year (not including benefits, payroll taxes, etc). The 1% of profits would allow 165,940 people to be hired with family wage jobs. According to the US Department of Commerce the average person making $50,000 or less spends about 38% of their paycheck on consumer items (used total average personal income and divided by personal consumption expenditures).[71] Take 38% of the $7.4 billion in new salaries and we get $2,837,586,648 that could be added to the consumer spending pool if these jobs were created. According to US economic business analysis the total for consumer spending in May 2013 was $10,690,000,000 for the quarter. The $2,837,586,648 in additional consumer spending (I divided that by four since this is for a 3 month period= $709,396,662) would equal a 6.6% increase in consumer spending just in that quarter. Now I realize these are simplistic numbers and thousands of factors go into how much could be infused into the US economy. We've already discussed how much our US economy improved when our consumer spending showed a mere 1% increase. Imagine what 6% would do? Would corporations get back their $7.4 billion investment through increased sales of consumer spending? Would the increase in spending grow financial markets (Wall Street) and increase what people save and invest? Would it increase the construction industry and home purchases? Would it allow more middle class families to realize the dream of higher education which fuels our future?

Smarter people than me could do years of research to determine the validity of this argument. We all know that large corporations will not take the same risks on job creation as they do with other risky business models like subpar mortgages, new product lines, or unethical practices which lead to gigantic law suits. For the purposes of this book in helping both large corporations and their workers stabilize the workplace to help grow the US economy, I believe that if larger corporations took these investments they would realize similar or flat growth in profits. But perhaps one more aspect of this investment needs to change, maybe Wall Street!

What would it take for Wall Street gurus to de-emphasize bottom line profits for strategies on job infrastructure and stability in consumer spending? What would happen if a company's stock price was directly related to their own contribution to national consumer spending and job creation? While our financial system continues to repeat the errors of faulty regulation; too big to fail banks that are only larger after the 2008 recession, and risky investments still taking place on the tax payer's back, perhaps it takes a dedicated optimist like myself to dream that one day corporations (who apparently are like people) will focus on their customer more than their bottom line.

This is a nice chart from Huffington Post on how banks have grown despite the problems they caused which ignited our recession in 2008.[72]

Too Big To Fail, Now Even Bigger

Since the collapse of Lehman Brothers in September 2008, the very biggest U.S. banks are now even bigger, with even more assets (in bank accounting, these are risks) relative to the size of the U.S. economy, meaning they could pose an even greater danger to the financial system.

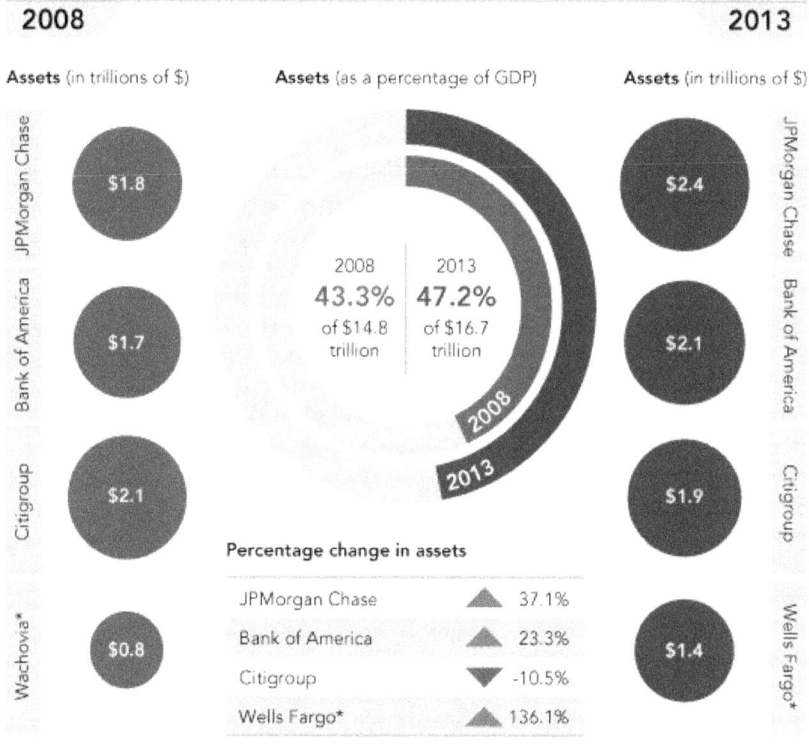

*Wachovia was absorbed by Wells Fargo in 2009.

Sources: Federal Reserve, Bureau of Economic Analysis   THE HUFFINGTON POST

Throughout US history the patterns of *downsizing* are consistent and in recent years are increasing. When looking at any decade of time since 1990, you can see clearly that job loss and consumer spending affect one another both positively and negatively. When job loss occurs and companies cut *middle class* workers, consumer spending is down or in a negative trend. Proven with extensive research this negative trend proves the economy as a whole suffers and higher job loss ensues. Remember that the main reason companies **downsize** is to improve financial performance. The next section covers more research that shows some companies don't improve at all, in fact, some get worse. But what would happen if companies avoided **downsizing** and the job loss rate reduces? What would happen if the *middle class* grew and their spending grew at the same rate? What would happen if consumer spending increased 1.5% or higher quarter after quarter? We know the history of what happens when the economy suffers a loss so we also know how many jobs can be created when our economy strengthens. Let's now take a look at how **downsizing** affects financial performance of corporations.

Important Points:

- In 2003, U.S. consumer spending accounted for around 70 percent of U.S. gross domestic product (GDP).[73]
- When consumer spending shrinks it affects every major business and household in the US.
- *Corporate profits stood at **14.2** percent in the third quarter of 2012, the **largest** share at any time since 1950, while the portion of income that went to employees was **61.7 percent**, near its lowest point since 1966.*[74]
- In 2010 the difference between the upper/middle class and the rest of us was 42%; a 45% decrease in wealth to 80% of the US population.
- *Middle-income Americans have seen their median net worth remain roughly flat over the past **quarter-century**, at $93,150 in 2010, compared to $91,056 in 1983.*[75]
- Upper income families *have seen their median net worth grow over the same period by 87 percent, to $574,788 from $307,134.*[76]
- The 1% of corporate profits reinvested could allow 165,940 people to be hired with family wage jobs.

RESULTS OF DOWNSIZING; FINANCIAL PERFORMANCE

Financial results for companies that have **downsized** have been a subject of much research and study. While there are some examples of companies improving, a significant number

of companies see diminished capacity both in size and financial performance over time. In a study from Paris University, companies with layoffs from three decades (1970-2001), 14 countries, and a total of 15,000 announcements *showed a negative effect on stock prices.*[77] According to an article by Worrell, Davidson, et. al in 1991, of 194 firms that announced layoffs during the period of 1979-1987, there was a *significantly negative market reaction to the announcements with the cumulative loss in stock value being about 2 % of the value.*[78] In 1994 authors De Meuse, Vanderheiden, and Bergmann conducted a large **downsizing** study of Fortune 100 companies where statistical tests revealed no significant positive relationships for any of the financial variables. The authors concluded that *empirical evidence did not support the contention that **downsizing** leads to improved financial performance.*[79] Authors Cascio, Young, and Morris studied financial data from the Standard & Poor (S&P) 500 between 1980 and 1994 and reported that *firms engaging in downsizing did not show significantly higher*

> *...firms with stable employment consistently outperformed companies with employment downsizing.*

returns than the average companies in their own industries.[80] In 1999 the same authors studied changes in employment from 1981 to 1992 and concluded *that firms with stable employment consistently outperformed companies with employment downsizing.*[81]

Before reaching the year 2000 many studies show significant data that disproves ***downsizing*** leads to improved financial performance. In 2004, Pittsburg State University Department of Economics concluded that ***downsizing*** *may have an adverse effect on job performance and correspondingly a negative impact on the financial performance of the organization.*[82] For the years 2000 and beyond let's examine a few companies that have conducted significant ***downsizing*** and review their financial performance over time:

Company	Stock Symbol	2000 Stock Price	2000 P/E Ratio	2013 Stock Price	2013 P/E Ratio
Cisco	CSCO	$65.50	109.00	$24.17	12.99
Best Buy	BBY	$27.50	34.71*	$34.06	13.28
Household Finance	HBC	$85.14*	Unavailable	$53.67	11.51
General Electric	GE	$57.81	47.00	$23.63	17.51

Source: [83 84 85 86 87 88 89 90 91 92] * 2004 data.

I worked for Best Buy from 2002 to 2005 and witnessed a gigantic change in the organization. At that time Circuit City was still a competitor but larger stores like Wal-Mart, Home Depot, and Target were expanding their technology departments to compete. I'll never forget a company management meeting around 2004 where the President of

Stores (at the time) Brian Dunn spoke to us about the biggest change the company will ever face. It was dramatic with videos and passionate speeches regarding how hard it is leave the past and forge ahead to a new and uncertain direction. I'll never forget the words he was screaming while his face grew redder, he said, *we must burn the bridge behind us, never look back, and embrace this change as our destiny*. One of the regional managers followed and gave an emotional speech about how he wanted to quit the company when he heard about the massive change. He spoke about his personal struggle with coming to grips with this change and how in time, it will help the organization get stronger and grow. Every manager was on the edge of their seat; wondering what change would occur and why it was so emotional and difficult for our main leaders. After much dramatic build up we learned that our change was to be more *Customer Centric*. This meant that Best Buy would analyze their business and redesign its stores to meet the demands of key segments.[93] Exactly one year later we were all on a company mandated conference call that told us the *Customer Centric* model was taking too long to pay for itself and the company would layoff managers. Since I left Best Buy in 2005, multiple layoffs took place. Thousands of people lost their jobs, dozens of stores have been closed, yet Best Buy is not outperforming as a result of their **downsizing**. Now let's compare Best Buy's lack of success to a retailer that *is* successful in consumer electronics; Costco.

Costco Wholesale is the second largest retailer in America. Costco has thrived over the last five years growing 39 percent in sales and its stock price has doubled since 2009.[94] Costco is well known for treating its employees well because they believe that a happier work environment will result in a more profitable company.[95] In an article entitled *Costco CEO Craig Jelinek Leads the Cheapest, Happiest Company in the World* reports Jelinek *earned $650,000 in 2012, plus a $200,000 bonus and stock options worth about $4 million, based on the company's performance.*[96]

... William Weldon, who took home $25.6 million which was more than three times the average CEO compensation while eliminating 9,000 jobs.

By contrast Brad Anderson, CEO of Best Buy earned $3.2 million in 2005 when Best Buy started its *downsizing*. His salary jumped to $49.3 Million in 2008 and when Brian Dunn took over during the recession his salary fell to $1.66 Million.[97] Before Jelinkek took over as CEO of Costco, Jim Sinegal was the CEO and co-founder. For his last year as CEO he was paid $350,000 for running a $70 billion company; twice the size of Best Buy.[98] While Best Buy continued to lay off people during the recession, Costco did not perform layoffs in 2009. Costco did place a freeze on hiring in its corporate offices and continued to hire as needed.[99]

So we can see a difference in employee philosophy and CEO pay between the two companies but what about electronics? When you buy computers or televisions from Best Buy you have a 14 day return policy and unless you buy an extended warranty, these electronic items are based on the manufactures warranty. Any issues with the product after 14 days you were stuck working with the manufacturer. When your item needs repair at Best Buy it can take weeks if not months in their Geek Squad service area to get your product in working order. There is normally a charge for such repairs. At Costco the return policy is generous and they double any manufactures' warranty. When there is an issue with a product you go directly to Costco for resolution. In addition Costco has set up a free technical support number for any questions you may have with your purchase. Customer satisfaction is higher at Costco then at Best Buy and the average employee makes almost double what Best Buy pays with greater benefits and more time off. So let's review what makes Costco successful; reasonable CEO pay, ease of shopping, positive employee focus, stands by their products, and avoided *downsizing* in 2009. In addition to these reasons Costco has one of the lowest turnover rates in all of retail. They provide a family wage job with health benefits to all employees. When you have a focused retail eye like me, it's important to point out another main reason why Costco succeeds over Best Buy; inventory levels and pricing. Many people believe that customer service is the key ingredient to making a retail operation successful. This is hard to argue but as consumer spending is trending towards stores that are self service, the number one key ingredient to being successful in retail is having the merchandise in stock. Generous supply of merchandise and low prices play a key role in Costco's success. And it's not just the amount of merchandise, it's the merchandise people want.

Another important rule of retail is the corporation that gets

your money first, gets more of your money. If you are going to Costco to buy a television, you will also buy groceries, towels, and other items out of convenience. That means you are less likely to go to Target, Wal-Mart, or other retailers for similar goods. Costco has their TVs stacked in huge quantities, rarely running out of inventory. If they are low on inventory their website provides free delivery to your door. As Costco continues to keep their employees and customers happy, they will outperform financially over an extended period of time. A report by the Retail Systems Research (RSR) entitled *The State of Retail Workforce Management*,[100] dated November 7th, 2007 states that *before frontline employees can be an effective part of these (customer centric) strategies, retailers need to move away from treating their workforce as a tool of customer service and more as an asset that, when invested in and managed well, responds in kind -- happy employees that make for happy customers.*[101]

Best Buy saw a negative business trend and they reacted quickly to reduce labor to show the company was being *responsible* to their shareholders. Unfortunately they were not responsible to their employees or customers which have perpetuated their downward trend for years. In 2009 Wayne F. Cascio wrote that *companies that conducted large-scale layoffs significantly underperformed compared with those that conducted few or no layoffs; with respect to profit margin, return on investment, return on equity, and total return on common stock.*[102]

While the research and evidence suggest a failure to produce improved financial performance as a result of *downsizing*, these corporations were able to  consistently improve one financial metric; <u>CEO pay</u>. Back in 1970, a minority of top executives made over **30 times** what their workers made. In 2009, the 17th annual Executive Excess states, *CEOs of major U.S. corporations averaged 263 times the average compensation of American workers* (the *middle class*).[103] Researchers at the University of Arkansas tracked the earnings of executives at major U.S. corporations who ordered 229 layoffs during the 1990s. A year after the layoff, the average total CEO compensation went up 23%.[104] The 17th annual executive compensation survey (2010) of CEO Pay by the Institute for Policy Studies shows that CEO salaries are double the 1990s CEO pay average.[105]

As we can see the CEO's of some large US corporations were getting significant raises that were outpacing their employees. If we are still to consider payroll as the largest controllable expense of any company, the CEO's pay became the largest expense of payroll that was seldom controlled. This would lead to future *downsizing* in order to afford the CEO's raises and keep the company profitable. What seems more complicated to understand is when CEO's are rewarded for *downsizing.* According to an article by Ann Binlot CEOs at 50 companies that lay off the most employees *took home an average pay of almost $12 million in 2009,* **42% more** *than the average CEO pay.*[106] The article goes on to say that *the $598 million compensation of the top 50 CEOs could provide average unemployment benefits for 37,759 workers for an entire year or nearly a month of benefits for each of the 531,363 employees laid off by those companies.*[107] If companies are *downsizing* because they need to save money in payroll why would they take payroll from thousands of workers and transfer it to a higher payroll expense with their CEO? One example from this report is Johnson & Johnson's William Weldon, who took home $25.6 million which was **more than three times** the average CEO compensation while eliminating 9,000 jobs.[108] The Huffington Post listed the top 10 CEO's from this study and their salaries and layoffs.[109] Here's a simple chart:

CEO	Company	The Year	Total Compensation	Total Layoffs
1. Fred Hassan	Schering-Plough	2009	$49,653,063	16,000
2. William Weldon	Johnson & Johnson	2009	$25,569,844	8,900
3. Mark Hurd	Hewlett Packard	2009	$24,201,448	6,400
4. Robert Iger	Walt Disney	2009	$21,578,471	3,400
5. Samuel Palmisano	IBM	2009	$21,159,289	7,800
6. Randall Stephenson	AT&T	2009	$20,244,312	12,300
7. Michael Duke	Walmart	2009	$19,234,269	13,350
8. Alan Mulally	Ford	2009	$17,916,654	4,700
9. Louis Chenevert	United Technologies	2009	$17,897,666	13,290
10. Ivan Seidenberg	Verizon	2009	$17,485,796	21,308

Source: Huffington Post Article, September 1st, 2010.[110]

Another chart from *Mother Jones* shows CEO pay increases from 2009 to 2010[111]:

Executive Company	CEO pay in 2010 Change vs. 2009	Meanwhile, workers take the hit...
Michael T. Duke *Walmart*	$18.7 million -4%*	13,000 jobs cut Ended longtime profit sharing program for low-level workers.
Jeffrey R. Immelt *General Electric*	$15.1 million +175%	17,000 jobs cut Also signaled that it will scale back pensions and health plan and may freeze wages.
Angela F. Braly *WellPoint*	$13.4 million +3%	3,000 jobs cut Nation's largest health insurer cut employee health benefits and capped days off.
Mark G. Parker *Nike*	$13.1 million +84%	1,750 jobs cut Spokesperson: "It's about realigning the business for the future."
Hugh Grant *Monsanto*	$12.4 million +15%	1,500 jobs cut Due in part to weaker demand for Roundup herbicide.
Craig Dubow *Gannett*	$7.9 million +80%	2,400 jobs cut Also continued policy of mandatory furloughs.
Clarence Otis, Jr. *Darden Restaurants*	$7.7 million +15%	5,000 jobs cut Owner of Olive Garden and Red Lobster undermines "no layoffs" image.
Gary M. Rodkin *ConAgra Foods*	$7.6 million +29%	1,200 jobs cut Plus 520 additional jobs to be cut at Slim Jim plant.
Keith E. Wandell *Harley Davidson*	$6.4 million +1%	1,000 jobs cut Froze wages, diluted benefits, and boosted use of low-paid temps.
Peter L. Lynch *Winn-Dixie*	$5.3 million +16%	2,000 jobs cut 30 grocery stores closed due to sales lost to Walmart.

Sources: *New York Times*, SEC filings, news clips

One argument to prevent high CEO pay would be to change the structure of their compensation. If they received incentives for bottom line performance then *downsizing* employees would spike up their profit due to slashing expenses. This would inflate their bonus which benefits the few; not the *middle class*. As we've seen previous examples of Costco CEO's salary proportional to their business and incentives based on stock performance are more equitable to the company and their employees.

CEO pay should be based on total company performance over time which should include stock performance, market share, turn over, customer satisfaction, and year over year sales growth.

RESULTS OF DOWNSIZING; PERSONAL WEALTH

We've examined the financial performance of corporations that have *downsized*. Their main focus is improving the financial health of their company even though this is not consistently realized. These companies should also consider the financial health of the affected employees who lose their job and the actual dollars that are lost. This negative income not only affects the individual families but the entire US economy. From 1992 to 2000 the Clinton Presidency brought greater incomes for all levels of the families. In 1992, it was reported that 10 million Americans were unemployed

...the average earnings were reduced to $1,910 per month—48 percent lower than their average pre-job earnings.

which resulted in an increase in poverty.[112] As noted in the President's report *family incomes were losing ground to inflation and jobs were being created at the slowest rate since the Great Depression.*[113] As a result of various economic policies President Clinton implemented his administration created *more than 22.5 million jobs. Of the total new jobs, 20.7 million, or 92 percent, were in the **private** sector.*[114] In 2012 Alan Krueger, a professor of Economics and Public Affairs at Princeton, notes that *if in the first decade of the 2000s the income of the median household had grown at the same rate as it did in the 1990s, middle-class households would have an extra $8,900 a year to spend on their mortgages, rent, cars, food and clothing, or to add to their savings.*[115] While an additional $742 a month may not seem a lot of money, for the *middle class* this money could be the difference of making a monthly mortgage payment or paying down debt. This amount would be significant to stabilizing the economy and strengthening consumer spending. While the $742 would be spent every month it would stabilize families and provide them more confidence and stability when considering buying goods and services.

Another important metric to study is how lower salaries or underemployment can affect *middle class* workers over time. Authors Davis and Wachter stated of the almost *7 million American workers displaced from long-term jobs* can generate a *total loss of earnings of roughly $774 billion over the next quarter century.*[116] Imagine what $744 Billion dollars of *additional* consumer spending would bring to the US economy?

The Hamilton project also analyzed salary loss as a result of **downsizing** during the time of October 2008 to April 2009 and determined *workers made roughly $3,640 per month, or $43,700 annually on average. Two years following their job loss, the average earnings of this group were reduced to $1,910 per month, about $23,000 annually—48 percent lower than their average pre-job earnings.*[117] Further studies have shown that *a worker who returns to work after long term unemployment* (people who have been unemployed for 12 months or longer) *will earn 20 percent less over the next 15 to 20 years than a worker who has continuous employment.*[118] From the Council of Economic Advisors to President Obama, *a total of $16 trillion in wealth was erased by the financial and housing crisis (of 2008), causing families to pull back on spending plans, and in turn leading companies to cut back hiring, lay off valued employees, and halt investment plans.*[119] Let's really think about this number, *$16 trillion*. If you were to magically get back the $16 Trillion dollars the US economy lost and used that money to pay off our national debt, our country would practically be **debt-**free.

In retail and in other industries your total compensation consists of a base salary, bonus potential, and general benefits. At Kohl's, a store manager makes base plus a 30% potential team bonus where the total company performance is measured to goal. During the recession years of 2008 and 2009 the company had good financial performance relative to the competition. The team bonus was paid. Kohl's is currently losing their customers to competitors like Macy's, Target, Ross, and Marshalls. As a result, team bonuses are smaller or nonexistent. What does this all mean to the manager? If you base your consumer spending on your total compensation and you don't receive a bonus it's as if you're getting a 30% pay cut. This will reduce confidence and stability in the family and constrict consumer spending. This not only affects *middle class* families but it lowers the sales expectations for Kohl's because the group that makes the most money of any position will buy less.

A person's **h**ealth should also be considered to be directly related to a person's **w**ealth. The psychological and health attributes of *downsizing* have also been studied. A study by Kivimäki, Vahtera, et al proves *that the threat of job loss generated by downsizing resulted in increased morbidity* (the incidence of disease).[120] A study by Bohle, Quinlan and Mayhew, in 2001 *concluded that 88% of the 68 studies identified found a measurable adverse, including an increased risk of work-related injury, occupational violence, cardiovascular disease and psychological distress/mental illness.*[121] [122] When a person's job is lost or threatened it can shatter confidence and stability and stress and uncertainty dominate a person's mind and body. Larger corporations may not consider the increased costs to employees as it relates to more frequent medical benefits being paid for conditions associated with *downsizing.* These costs are not just for those who are *downsized* but those employees that remain will also show increased incidence rates of illness and loss of productivity. Another study in 2004 of middle-aged managers by Strazdins, D'Souza, et al found that *the effects of downsizing resulted in markedly higher odds of mental and physical health problems.*[123] [124] One example shows a group of Nurses that were *downsized* exhibited *anger, emotional exhaustion, and distress* which are all indicators of depression.[125] As illness increases as a result of *downsizing,* so do the costs to society who pays for emergency room visits not covered due to lack of insurance.

Important Points:

- Companies with layoffs from three decades (1970-2001), 14 countries, and a total of 15,000 announcements *showed a negative effect on stock prices.*[126]
- *Empirical evidence did not support the contention that* **downsizing** *leads to improved financial performance.*[127]
- *Companies that conducted large-scale layoffs significantly underperformed compared with those that conducted few or no layoffs.*[128]
- *CEOs of major U.S. corporations averaged 263 times the average compensation of American workers* (the *middle class*).[129]
- *A worker who returns to work after long term unemployment will earn 20 percent less over the next 15 to 20 years than a worker who has continuous employment.*[130]

For all the research that documents downsizing, it typically does not lead to improved financial performance. Let's provide insight to how corporations can avoid *downsizing*. The article *Alternatives for Downsizing* lists 50 ways for companies to avoid the harmful effects of *downsizing*. Some ways to avoid *downsizing* are as follows: employee incentives for identification of cost savings; eliminate expense accounts or mileage payments; invest in employee health and wellness to increase performance; and productivity or leave vacant positions unfilled.[131] Other strategies to avoid *downsizing* include the creation of new workflows/teams, lend or transfer employees to other companies (we'll talk about this later in the book; look for up-sizing.com), ask employees to identify ways to meet dollar amount of reductions needed, ask your customers and suppliers how to reduce costs and improve performance and productivity, and sell company assets to raise cash.[132] GE encouraged hourly worker reviews of operational performance measures which not only helped solve complex problems but improved the working experience of the front line operators.[133]

> *...the economy cannot possibly get out of its current doldrums without a strategy to revive the purchasing power of America's vast middle class.*

In addition to avoiding ***downsizing*** many examples have been provided to help improve economic class inequality. Robert Reich, professor of public policy at University of California, Berkeley and Labor Secretary under Bill Clinton wrote in 2012 how inequality could improve in the US. Some of his suggestions included *having unemployment insurance cover part-time work, giving transition assistance to move to new jobs in new locations* (which we'll talk about later in this book), *creating insurance for communities that lost a major employer, have Medicare available to anyone, have big companies pay severance to American workers they let go and train them for new jobs, increase minimum wage to half of the median wage, and we could have insisted that the foreign nations we trade with do the same, so that all citizens could share in gains from trade.*[134] While this problem may seem too complex or idealistic to solve other countries have experienced similar growth avoiding most class inequality. Robert Reich uses Germany as an example stating, …*while Americans' average hourly pay has risen only 6 percent since 1985, German workers' pay has risen almost 30 percent.*[135] Reich believes as I've stated so far that consumer spending is necessary to not only repair the US economy but to lessen inequality amongst the economic classes. He writes: *the economy cannot possibly get out of its current doldrums without a strategy to revive the purchasing power of America's vast middle class. The spending of the richest 5 percent alone will not lead to a virtuous cycle of more jobs and higher living standards.*[136] To find out more about inequality and Robert Reich please see his movie *Inequality for All.*

Professors Edmund Phelps and Leo Tilman, at Columbia University, *have proposed the creation of a National Innovation Bank that would invest in, or lend to, innovative start-ups — bringing more money to bear than venture-capital funds could, and at a lower cost of capital, which would promote more investment and enable the funding of somewhat riskier ventures.*[137] It is well known that innovation has grown our economy in the past and can be a good source of job creation. Another pursuit than can improve class mobility is higher education. Throughout this book and as evidenced in countless research papers, the more education you have, the more employable you'll become over time. As innovation and technology improve, it will require more skills and instruction from higher education sources. Obtaining this education through colleges or trade schools will allow *middle class* workers to realize higher paying jobs. A survey by the National Employment Law Project states that *three-quarters of American job growth in 2010 came within industries paying less than $15 an hour.*[138] If this trend continues and education remains low, the *middle class* will shrink down even further and poverty in the US will grow. While we will always have jobs in the lower end of wage categories, we can work with our local governments to encourage raising the minimum wage and allowing more struggling families the opportunity to earn wages that match the increase of goods and services we discussed earlier. A higher minimum wage would potentially reduce economic class inequality and allow those on the lower end of the spectrum an opportunity for economic mobility.

Too often larger corporations communicate solely from the top down. This alienates employees from the decision making process and eliminates their expertise dealing with products, services, and the all important customer. Employees have key insight being on the ground floor working side by side with opportunities each corporation faces. Often managers will isolate themselves in a conference room to mull over ideas that could help the business, save them money, or increase sales. While managers could possess higher education and a higher level of forward thinking, they cannot master customer feedback like your average worker. It is therefore important for corporations to utilize employee lead groups that encourage ideas, participation, and creative thinking to help the company, and themselves secure their jobs. Meetings can be scheduled in addition to providing the employees a web site to post ideas, customer issues, and resolutions to key opportunities the company is facing. Once the employees are regularly allowed to offer suggestions to improve performance, it is up to the company to provide the results of their efforts. Vince Lombardi, one of the greatest coaches of all time, said *If winning isn't everything, why do they keep score*? The more results the company can show to their employees, the more the employees will see that they are winning and they are directly tied to the company's success. These results can also help employees realize the importance of their own productivity and how it relates to job stabilization and overall company performance. Employee empowerment provides many benefits to the company, their families, and the US economy as a whole. Another type of reward can be a contest involving gifts, a paid day off, dinner for the family, or a financial bonus to incentivize employees to be diligent in improving performance, cutting costs, and saving jobs. Employees are often encouraged by contests and prizes that draw their competitive nature to solve the most complex and serious problems. The reward is also a form of recognition which is commonly cited as one of the most effective tools for maintaining a positive working environment. And, as we've seen in Costco's example: a positive working environment produces outstanding financial performance.

Another way for corporations to avoid ***downsizing*** is by *insourcing*. One example is GE's *insourcing* of appliance manufacturing to the U.S. *by increasing manufacturing capability and bringing manufacturing jobs back to the U.S. from Korea, China, and Mexico.*[139] Their $1 billion plan needed to reduce new product development cycles from 3 to 4 years to 1 to 1.5 years. This included major repairs, new work teams, training and development, and an investment in new product lines. According to the Harvard Business Review article by Brad Power, *GE management decided to bring production of a water heater back to the U.S. from an Asian contractor* which resulted in *a new design, with better performance: 20% fewer parts and 50% less labor. Inventory was reduced 60%, labor efficiency improved 30%, time-to-produce was reduced 68%, and space required for the line came down by 80%.*[140] GE filled their empty plants in Louisville, Kentucky with American workers. GE was able to improve their profit and performance by creating jobs in the US. This is a critical success story that should motivate other corporations to look for ways to reduce costs and improve productivity to allow the creation of US jobs at family wages. Over time more companies like GE can realize their overall performance improvement as well as giving the US economy a well deserved positive push in the growth direction.

Another example of *insourcing* is by General Motors. General Motors' first generation of *insourcing* will result in the hiring of 10,000 technology professionals.[141] An article by Stephanie Overby states *many CIO's* (Chief Information

Officers) *are reconsidering the outsource-insource mix, particularly in the manufacturing industry.*[142] As you may know one of the key problems in our economy is when manufacturing jobs get shipped overseas. This can devastate small towns where manufacturers live. It also takes highly paid workers and forces them into an economy with low wage jobs. The more manufactures' re-invest in the US economy, the more stable their work force will be and the stability of communities they live in will grow and stay strong. Mark Compton Deputy Director of Online Content for the White House states that *large manufacturers like Ford and Caterpillar have announced large investments in U.S. facilities.*[143] Where I live, KEEN, the footwear designer, opened a 15,000-square-foot facility to manufacture boots moving production from China to a location just five miles from its corporate headquarters in Portland, Oregon.[144]

President Obama will put forward new tax proposals to create incentives for businesses to invest in hiring and expanding in the US. In addition, the President's plan will provide the financial and technical support necessary for companies to grow and expand in the US.[145] There is also current legislation to promote *insourcing* to US companies called the 'Senate Immigration Bill" where foreign outsourcing firms will need to pay more thereby discouraging outsourcing.[146] This bill will also limit temporary visas for corporations to further encourage creating jobs here in the US.

Corporations must also consider changing lower wage jobs to family wage jobs. While California and other states are moving this through their legislative process, more of the country needs to realize that while your employment expense will go up, you are providing *middle class* workers more money to spend in our economy. The corporation is also stabilizing the *middle class* worker which will result in greater productivity and longer tenure at your company. And an increase in consumer spending positively affects Wall Street, your stock price, and your overall financial performance. Unions have provided leadership and assistance in helping the *middle class* gain family wage jobs.

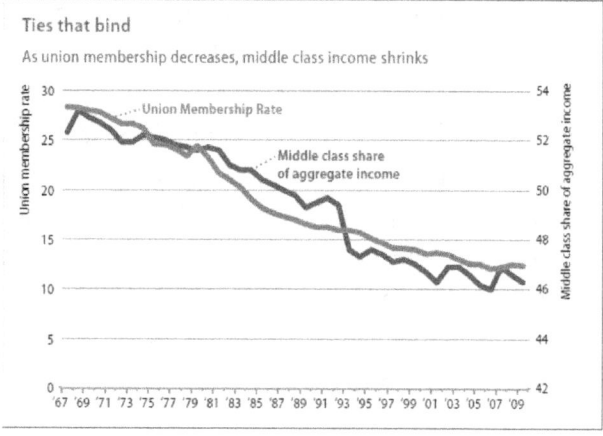

Sources: Authors' analysis. Union Membership rate is from Barry T. Hirsch, David A. Macpherson, and Wayne G. Vroman, "Estimates of Union Density by State." Middle Class Share of Aggregate Income is from United States Census Bureau.

Ties that bind

As union membership decreases, middle class income shrinks

Union Membership Rate

Middle class share of aggregate income

147

As the above chart shows when union membership decreases so does the *middle class*. A report entitled *Unions Make the Middle Class* shows that *every percentage point increase of union membership, puts about $153 more in the pockets of the middle class worker.*[148] While this amount may seem small, the report goes on to document that *Union workers on average earn 15% more than non-union workers.* [149] [150] According to the Center for American Progress, *less than 12% of all workers are currently union members,* and should *care about this decline because unions give workers a bigger say in our economy and our political system.*[151] Unions have lobby power similar to those of large corporations and can negotiate higher wages, better benefits, and decrease *downsizing.* Bruce Western from Harvard University and Jake Rosenfeld of Washington University conducted a study that showed *private sector union membership in the United States declined from 34 to 8 percent for men and from 16 to 6 percent for women. During this period, inequality in hourly wages increased by over 40 percent.*[152] Unions are responsible for *the largest career training program outside the military* via their apprenticeship programs.[153] Unions are also integrated with the communities they serve. Donna Brazile of CNN states *union letter carriers save lives all the time by alerting officials when an elderly person hasn't collected his or her mail from the mailbox and union members arranged haircuts for more than 700 kids going back to school.*[154] As we've seen in community efforts and wages, unions influence non-union members as well which can help stabilize the US economy.

More union involvement suggests improvement in average wages, economic class inequality, and overall consumer spending. It goes without saying that Unions have become more controversial with far right politicians passing legislation to eliminate unions and limit their impact on corporate America. While these politicians are saving their corporate donors considerable cash, we've already learned that this cash is not re-invested in our US economy or our communities. It appears that some of these savings go to the CEO's. Kevin Drum from Mother Jones' writes *If unions had remained strong … over the past three decades likely would have grown at about the same rate as the overall economy—just as they had in the postwar era. But they didn't,* thus t*he entire bottom 80 percent now loses a collective $743 billion each year and the top 1 percent gains $673 billion.*[155]

While it's difficult for unions to compete with gigantic corporate cash pouring to politicians and lobbyists, they do have a long history of providing the *middle class* with higher wages and reduce economic class inequality.

For myself, being in the corporate world for three decades, I too have evidenced based, proven ideas to avoid *downsizing*. I've found that a strategic planning effort is a great place to start. Strategic planning is considered to be a proactive approach for companies to assess their opportunities and plan for improvement versus a knee jerk reaction to cut expenses through *downsizing*. De Meuse who studied *downsizing* in 2004 suggests a more proactive approach makes it more likely for corporations to succeed.[156]

STRATEGIC PLANNING

The strict definition of strategic planning is a *systematic process of envisioning a desired future, and translating this*

vision into broadly defined goals or objectives and a sequence of steps to achieve them.[157] Before getting into specific strategies let me say as a consultant for 19 years how much I condemn traditional strategic planning efforts. Some consulting firms can take 6 to 12 months to develop a strategic plan. Other than generating fees how is this approach *strategic*? In my professional view if you take longer than 60 days to create a strategic plan, the economy and industry metrics you're studying will be ancient history and not relevant to the strategic plan. If the main purpose of the plan is to create goals and objectives that are *achievable*, then the plan must stay current and relevant. During those 60 days you uncover the truths about your organization from many different perspectives. This can be done using a needs assessment which we'll talk about soon. With that information you have the ability to create simple, measureable, and reasonable goals for the organization to achieve. The goals will be created, agreed upon, and should be monitored every 30 days. This allows the strategic planning process to be fluid and adaptable to change. As markets change or conditions change the organization can adapt quickly, redefine goals if necessary, and continue to monitor progress towards accomplishing their goals.

In order to start the process we need to ensure that every employee, customer, manager, board member, and stake holder has consensus on what opportunities are facing the corporation. It's critical to identify the correct set of problems without jumping to conclusions. But many corporations argue that their business issues are critical and cannot wait for a planning process. It's well known that *downsizing* is a 10 minute phone call versus other strategic plans that can take months or years. The purpose of my 60 day strategy is to provide corporations a quicker way to get to solutions to retain their people instead of eliminating them. Employees have a deep understanding and commitment to what they're doing and can be encouraged to find solutions senior management may not see. Getting feedback or needs assessment can be quick. Analyzing that data and formulating a plan can take some time but it does not have to take forever. The effects of quick *downsizing* have already been proven to be short lived financial improvement and usually suggest greater costs and weakened financial performance over time. By defining the problem with feedback and creating a meaningful, executable plan to fix it, strategic planning requires less time and less expense than most large scale *downsizing* strategies. My four-step approach starts with consensus or *being on the same page.*

STEP 1: BEING ON THE SAME PAGE:

Forbes magazine describes the two steps of strategic planning to **determine where you are** and identify **what's important.**[158] We talked about the importance of finding out **what's important** to your employees and your customers. This reminds me of a great time in my career when I worked for Bed, Bath, and Beyond. One day our Vice President spoke in a meeting and presented us with a new item; a $1,000 goose down feather pillow. While most managers in the meeting were taken aback by this expensive item they were also quick to dismiss its potential in our store. At the time I was in charge of the linens department, I saw this opportunity as a challenge, not impossible. I know full well that if you can find out what's important to a customer; you can sell anything. One day a businessman walked in my department and asked me *where your best pillows are*? I was quick to respond; *our best pillows or most expensive pillows*? The customer answered quickly and said *aren't they the same things*? This gave me my opportunity to present the $1,000 pillow. At first the customer was surprised by the amount of the pillow. After explaining some of the features of this pillow I noticed he was wearing a nice suit.

> *...you can sell anything to anyone when you know what is important.*

Since I had a background in men's suits from my dad's business, I asked if the he had a favorite suit. The customer smiled, looked me in the eye and said yes, of course, I love my blue suit, it's fabulous. As he glowed describing his suit I asked him if it was expensive and he quickly responded *yes*. I then asked him how many times he wore the suit and he responded *about once or twice a year*. Quickly analyzing his words and non verbal queues I had a pretty good idea that quality was important to him. I was ready to ask him the closing question. I stood up tall, gathered myself, looked him in the eye and asked him, *if you only wear this great suit once or twice, how often will you use this pillow*? We shared a blank stare at each other for a good 15 seconds he smiled at me and said those amazing words: *I'll take two of these $1,000 pillows*. This story, which I tell often, is proof that you can solve (or sell) any solution when you know what is ***important*** to that person. Another example of how this can be used is to obtain the information of what's important through a thoughtful and simple needs assessment. In order to see if the organization, the people they serve, and the community at large are all on the ***same page***, it's critical to ask the right questions to a variety of audiences and stakeholders. The more variety you include, the more consensus can be built. Examples of some questions can include:

1. Describe the need your organization addresses.
2. Can board members describe the core programs, who they serve, and the intended outcomes?
3. What is the current climate and how is it affecting our customers and our organization?
4. What three things motivate our staff?
5. What is the most important priority to address over the next 12 months?

6. Are sufficient resources allocated to ensure each program can achieve the established goals and objectives?
7. What are the performance indicators to ensure that the program meets its goals and objectives?
8. List three ideas that will advance the organization's cause or mission in the community?
9. List three things that concern you the most about this organization.
10. If money was no object what initiative would you like to start to improve your organization and the people you serve?

These questions and more will align everyone to a common goal; *being on the same page*. You can't move forward without this simple yet important step. The needs assessment will not only uncover strategies and goals, but suggest systems that needs to be in place to track performance over specific points of time. The performance results, or scores, are critical to every employee to visualize their progress towards the goals of the company. You don't know if you're winning if you don't keep score.

STEP 2: THREE GOALS:

There is an unspoken rule of three in comedy. It refers to three references or repetitions to increase laughter from an audience. At the end of the needs assessment you should develop three goals. While you can add more goals once the original three are exceeded, they should not consist of more than three at any other time. I've found throughout my years in management that giving a team any more than three priorities or goals can become unclear and difficult to implement. These goals are how the organization can *keep score* or track performance in order to see if they are accomplishing what they set out to do. I've seen some plans with ten goals and it adds a complexity that can frustrate people and take the organization off course.

Another major difference in my approach is I use evidenced-based research to determine what the goals should be. While it's important to consider the needs assessment for goal development, it's critical to conduct research to determine specific trends in the marketplace and what those trends suggest is an achievable goal. This allows the goals and the organization to be on the *same page* with widely used economic trends and best practices developed by successful companies or large industries. These trends include economic markets, competition, customer focus groups, emerging products, academic research on future trends, and government legislation or future trends. Without these details, goals can be meaningless.

STEP 3: WHO'S IN CHARGE?

You can't have a successful strategic plan without accountability. There could be a number of people or a committee that is in charge of monitoring goals and the overall climate of the market place. Clearly defined leadership roles and infrastructure are the tools that *implement* a strategic plan. Forbes magazine describes another step to strategic planning to **determine who is accountable**.[159] Those responsible for being in charge of this process must communicate effectively, decide how to allocate resources, and maintain specific measurements to ensure all of the goals are being met. What makes this step difficult is many people in the organization, regardless of title or rank, can redefine leadership and change course. At times management and boards can clash affecting the leadership of the organization and the overall goals everyone is trying to achieve. Others in senior management positions can disengage from one leader's direction and create their own direction causing conflict and confusion.

Phil Jackson is probably one of the greatest basketball coaches of all time. Imagine how many rings he would own if his leadership was constantly redefined by the players, senior management, and the fans. While Phil Jackson may take all levels of feedback to determine his leadership direction, that final direction comes from one person and one person only; Phil Jackson. Organizations must ensure that one person is ultimately accountable for the outcomes of a strategic plan. Without clear leadership, the plan cannot be implemented.

The burden of leadership can frequently take a toll on a manager or employee. I recommend changing leadership roles every three to six months. This will allow new perspectives on the corporations' progress and prevent leadership burn-out. It's critical that accountability remains vibrant and unburdened. The strategic plan gives the direction and refreshing leadership from time to time keeps accountability consistent.

Forbes magazine emphasizes that strategic planning **is never over**.[160] Oversight must continue every 30 days to ensure goals are being met and the market place remains constant. At the end of a six-month period the team should plan a half-day retreat to review the plan and the level of success of each goal achieved. The cost of this retreat must be modest and prove valuable to the company. The market should be analyzed again, different questions may be asked, and the process should start over again. Why? A strategic plan should stay relevant and not just sit on a shelf. Even if maximum success is achieved, there could be new emerging trends that can take your organization even further. The bottom line here is when a corporation implements a successful strategic plan; they can improve company performance and avoid the need to *downsize*. The moment an organization stops changing or growing is the moment that organization is *dead*.

Here is an example of a strategic plan for a nonprofit drug treatment organization. Many people in the organization had ideas of how to grow their business. We conducted a needs assessment and asked employees, board members, and our clients for suggestions on how we could approve. Some ideas from management were to spend money on remodeling, others wanted to negotiate contracts with county, state, and federal offices, and some wanted to eliminate services. All of these ideas were developed without the appropriate research to determine the best course of action based on *facts* not just ideology. When I began some evidenced based research I discovered

> ...*the moment an organization stops changing or growing is the moment that organization is dead.*

that while drug abuse and alcohol abuse increase slightly over time, treatment on a national level is not growing. The number of persons with substance dependence or abuse was stable between 2002 and 2009 (22.0 million in 2002, 21.6 million in 2003, 22.5 million in 2004, 22.2 million in 2005, 22.6 million in 2006, 22.3 million in 2007, 22.2 million in 2008, and 22.5 million in 2009).[161] Although the number of persons receiving substance abuse treatment within the past year remained stable between 2008 (4.0 million) and 2009 (4.3 million), the number increased between 2002 (3.5 million) and 2009.[162] In addition to researching drug use it's critical to research any government activity pertaining to funding of health and human services. I discovered that current legislation threatened to reduce the organizations income by $1.7 million, almost one-third of their revenue budget. The Aging & Disability Services Administration (ADSA) elimination of key programs could affect 55,000 people in the state. Another key research indicator for any substance abuse program is poverty. Local unemployment in March 2011 was 10.7% compared to the State rate of 9.7%.[163] According to the AP Economic Stress Index, the local county had the second highest economic stress index level in the state, factoring in unemployment, bankruptcy and foreclosure rates.[164]

With all of these indicators in place it was clear that the strategies being suggested by staff would not adequately address the financial problems of the organization. Based on the small amount of research I uncovered, the following suggestions could be implemented for improved results:

1. Maintain consistent level of occupancy in existing programs.
2. Explore preventative services that will have increased funding from the Affordable Care Act.
3. Explore new revenue streams that are not dependent on government spending.
4. Reduce operational expenses (not payroll) where appropriate.
5. Obtain agreement with vendors and past due accounts to lower monthly payments to build cash equity in the organization for better maneuvering.

While the following example is a short description of a complex process it does illustrate the importance for a needs assessment and the appropriate level of evidenced based research to properly lead an organization to improved financial performance. In addition to strategic planning, larger corporations must start investing their dollars in the majority of their people, not just the CEO.

INVEST MONEY WITH YOUR PEOPLE:

The next simple approach for corporations to avoid *downsizing* and the effect it has on their employees is to invest their money in people. Why is this important? As we discussed and have proven with evidenced based research, those corporations that eliminate thousands of jobs not only hurt the US economy but hurt their own business in the process. Any time a corporation directly or indirectly lowers consumer spending through job loss, their business will suffer financially. As we've discussed *downsizing* shrinks consumer spending and the market place which pulls capital out of 70% of the economy. Every corporation has a set of expenses associated with *downsizing*. Every corporation has projected savings from *downsizing*. Take both numbers and invest that money in the following ways:

INVEST IN JOB PLACEMENT:

If a corporation invests their money in job placement services for their displaced employees it can improve that corporation's long-term financial performance and stabilize the US economy. What I'm trying to show here is that corporations can take costs they're already anticipating and invest them into helping their employees with new jobs. I will be able to show that corporations will not spend more engaging in this process but could spend the same if not less. The typical costs of downsizing can include unemployment benefits, accrued time, severance pay, covering the responsibilities of the replaced position (including training costs and overtime), fees for a labor attorney, health insurance, and other ordinary expenses associated with restructuring or *downsizing*.[165] While it's difficult to put a dollar number considering all these variables let's see if we can compare it to the cost of relocating an employee to secure another job. According to the Worldwide ERC 2011 US Transfer Volume & Cost Survey the average relocation cost of a current employee that owns a home is $90,081 and the average relocation cost of a current employee that rents is $23,497.[166] Another cost that is extensively reviewed is involuntary turnover after *downsizing* has occurred. The employees that survive get nervous and look for other opportunities, and leave. Turnover can represent a significant hidden cost to corporations. Turnover costs include productivity losses during training, recruiting and lost work while a position is vacant. The April 2008 issue of the Academy of Management Journal states, *layoffs targeting just 1% of the workforce preceded, on average, a 31% increase in turnover*.[167] While the various variables of *downsizing* expenses are hard to detail, the cost of turnover is clearer and highly researched. A 2012 article by Suzanne Lucas states *for all jobs earning less than $50,000 per year, the average cost of replacing an employee amounts to 20 percent of the person's annual salary*, while those jobs that are *lower-paying (those under $30,000 a year) at 16 percent of annual salary*.[168] An example from this article shows *37 percent of hotel/motel and food services employees voluntarily quit a job in 2011* which represents a large expense.[169] Let's see if we can extrapolate the math:

According to the US Census Bureau the number of employees (as of 2008) in this employment segment with companies that report payroll was 11,926,000.[170] Now let's take 37% of this number or 4,412,620. The US Census Bureau calculates the payroll for this employment segment at $183.2 billion or an average of $15,361 annual salary per employee.[171] Now we can take the 4,412,620 employees who voluntarily quit and multiply that by the average annual salary of $15,361 and you get $67.7 billion. Take that number and multiply it by 16% (an average cost of replacing these lower paid employees) and you get a total estimated cost of $10.8 billion for voluntary turn over for this specific segment. What an amazing number! Now if we divide the $10.8 billion by the 4,412,620 affected employees we get a dollar amount of $2,447.52 per employee who leaves voluntarily. If you take the 16% of their average annual salary as the cost for relocation for another job you would get a total of $2,457.76. That leaves the employee or the company needing another *$10.24* to relocate and find a new job. We've proven the cost-savings from assisting current employees in relocating to help them retain their job. Imagine if corporations in this employment segment avoided **downsizing** (of any kind) and were able to reduce their turn over by just 20%. That would save this employment segment $2.7 billion in costs. What investments or development can be done with $2.7 billion? Not to mention if this savings were invested into better working relationships with employees and customers.

I'm confident that if any corporation compares these average costs to the costs mentioned above they could either break even or save money by investing resources to relocate an employee to another employer. In an ideal world it would be nice to have a network of companies that have hiring needs at our finger tips. It would be nice to quickly find one company willing to take 500 employees from another company and fulfill their need of 500 employees for a new location. While this simple system

Downsizing by Brad S. Lebowsky

may not exist, corporations have resources to determine where their employees can go to work. That way, unemployment does not rise, the US economy is not affected, the company is communicating a strong message that it supports its employees, and another company (competitor or not) can reduce costs by hiring workers that have a track record for reliability and performance. Now I realize that moving has a lot of factors such as schools, the employment considerations of a spouse, the condition or market value of a home, and family obligations. My point is to suggest that corporations can avoid *downsizing* by transferring their employees to another company, city, or state. How would this transfer work? Here is my idea:

Each employer by industry registers on a national website. Their email address and company information are stored and will receive regular updates on employment opportunities, employment activities, and the savings employers are realizing from this system. Employers who are reducing pay or eliminated jobs of 20 people or more can log into a site called **up-sizing.com** (the opposite of *downsizing)*. Next the employer sets up a **group** within the website for employees affected (20-20,000). Each employee will have a dedicated link that shows their pertinent information, years on the job, specific skills or training, education, performance reviews, and a one page resume. The concept is to group employees together to encourage other companies to acquire entire groups of affected employees. Once this information is loaded to the system, it is available for any large employer to access.

Let's say ABC Manufacturing wants to lay off 50 works due to a project that is closing down. Those 50 workers will be one group within the manufacturing segment of the website. XYZ manufacturing in another city or state is growing and wants to open another production line. They need 50 workers to get things started. XYZ manufacturing goes on the website and writes in their needs. An e-mail alert would be sent showing XYZ manufacturing the group of workers from ABC Manufacturing. XYZ manufacturing goes onto the website, finds this group of qualified people, reviews their skills and performance, and hires them all. The costs of relocation and recruiting can be negotiated between both manufactures. While the idea is simple it can create some difficulties.

Some manufacturers may want to hire locally to help their specific town or local economy. While arguments could be made that relocating talent to their specific town will help with their economy, I understand local businesses wanting to help local employees. One possible solution for this issue is to have groups of 10 employees segmented so a company can hire half from up-sizing.com and the other half from their local community. In addition to this site corporations can create an employee fund that can help finance job transfers and relocations.

If I were to create a dream consulting concept it would attract large companies considering *downsizing*. They would pay me $5 Million (I did say dream concept) for one year of consulting to help avoid *downsizing*. $2.5 Million would have to come out of the CEO's pay. If the company is failing to perform and unable to maintain its workforce, then it should directly affect the CEO's compensation as we discussed earlier. $4.9 Million of the $5 Million will be placed in an employee development and relocation fund. The fund would be managed by five employees, two board members, and three managers of the company. This group of ten people can allocate the funds for training, relocation, or other employee related needs. I would keep $100,000 for my consulting work in helping them develop this process.

INVEST IN JOB TRAINING AND DEVELOPMENT:

According to a 2013 study done by Martin and Davis states that *a focus on training and development can be expected to increase the knowledge and skills of individual employees to find ways to cut costs, improve efficiency, and enhance profitability.*[172] Sometimes the best people to solve a problem are the people who work for you. Corporations that experience a downturn in revenue or profits should consider training their employees to help solve the problem. One of my favorite stories from college is when a professor told me about a health club organization that had high level meetings with all of the Vice Presidents of the company to figure out a way to save money. Their operations were turning an operating loss and the President needed ideas to reduce costs quickly. After days of meetings the Vice Presidents were at a loss. At the end of one of these stressful and unproductive meetings one of the Vice Presidents went to one of their health club locations. He was disturbed by the lack of progress made to save the company money. He thought he would release some of his frustrations with a healthy workout. After the workout he saw Bob at the front of the showers. Bob was a loyal employee for over 10 years and his job was to hand guest towels. Bob warmly greeted the Vice President and noted he was not happy. Bob inquired about his frustration and Vice President told him about the meetings. With just a quick exchange the Vice President asked Bob *so tell me Bob,*

what things you would do to save money? Bob thought about for a minute and told the Vice President about the lotions and shampoo supplies he has to replenish multiple times a day. Bob thought this
could be source of rising expenses. The Vice President was pleased that Bob was able to identify something specific but was still unaware of a solution so he asked Bob *how we should solve this.* Bob quickly replied *remove the caps.* A lengthy pause took place as the Vice President required time to process such a simple and practical idea. In a way he was stunned and asked Bob again *what should we do?* Bob replied again *remove the caps.* Needless to say the Vice President was encouraged and reported to the board room the next day to share Bob's idea. As a result of this simple cost cutting measure and other ideas, the corporation saved $2.2 Million in expenses and avoided any loss of jobs. There are two reasons why I love this story: (1) employees are the most powerful allies to any corporation. If we win, they win and (2) when the idea is so simple and practical it's easy to implement and simple to track progress via results or *keeping score.*

In addition to tasking employees with problem solving duties the corporation can implement training efforts to improve the production and efficiency of their workers or train them for different industries. According to the 2011 article *Unemployment and Earnings Losses, for many of the nation's dislocated workers, counseling and training in high return areas, such as information technology, science, or emerging service sectors such as hospitality and retail, can help prepare them for jobs with earnings comparable to their previous position.*[173]

ALL EXPENSES MUST BE *PROPORTIONAL*:

Corporations *downsize* to quickly realize savings by cutting expenses. As discussed previously payroll is the largest controllable expense of most companies other than real estate. We've also discussed that not so popular but evident trend of CEO pay out pacing pay of *middle class* workers. We've even seen failing companies pay their CEOs above the national average. In 1994 when I completed and defended my Master's Thesis, I knew I would use this strategy throughout my personal and professional life; *Proportions*. Another way to look at *proportions* is a way to set priorities. In my personal life, I focus my energy and resources toward what is truly important; my priorities. While I may not keep the cleanest house in the block, nor do I drive the newest car on the block, I'm one of the few parents that provide my children with a free college education, a free car, and a way to secure a career after college. I also provide various opportunities to travel and explore our world. I guess it's one way to say *I put my money where my mouth is*. If a corporation, including CEO pay, is out of proportion to their business model then regardless of any *downsizing* activities, the financial performance will always be constrained.

To illustrate a basic example of *proportions* I recall a time shortly after obtaining my MBA. A large school district with a $330 Million budget asked for volunteers to analyze their budget. I was young, newly graduated, and unemployed so I thought this was a perfect opportunity to test out my theory. When I came to their district office to obtain the budget I asked them about their mission statement. They responded in dismay and said "what does our mission statement have to do with our budget?" I quickly replied, "It has **everything** to do with your budget". They responded by telling me that their mission was to strengthen the relationships between students, teachers, and parents. Knowing their organizational mission I quickly went to work categorizing their expenses. Not after too long I concluded that 57% of their expenses were involving maintenance and had nothing to do with their mission. In fact less than 30% of their overall budget was dedicated to their mission. My first of many suggestions was to limit their maintenance expense creatively or through securing a third-party company who can maintain the schools more efficiently and with less expense. Typically the third party company would hire existing staff to reduce or eliminate any *downsizing*. This would allow more resources to teachers and counselors which would strengthen their ability to meet their mission. Since it is my philosophy those budgets' resources are *proportioned* to support *human capital* or people in order to succeed in its mission, this suggestion would help the school district better align their resources.

Peter Cappelli from the University of Pennsylvania's Wharton School, and a leading expert on layoffs says *most (CEO's) have absolutely no idea if cutting employees is a good strategy. They don't have a systematic way to assess what is the net present value of the decision whether or not to lay people off, yet these same executives can make detailed calculations for virtually every other decision that comes across their desks.*[174] This is a critical point for every corporation to consider. If payroll is your largest expense then your employees are your largest catalyst to making your business successful.

The calculations presented in this book and the lessons we've learned from evidence-based research provide ample support that CEO pay can create an insurmountable burden on a corporation's financial performance. And when re-investing dollars away from the CEO to *middle class* employees, it not only improves the performance of the corporation but positively affects consumer spending and the US economy.

CEOs all have bonus structures and within that bonus structure should be financial rewards for avoiding *downsizing*. And if the CEO or top tier pay exceeds a reasonable *proportion* then it should be reinvested for infrastructure, job training, or relocation services. We've now discussed several ways for corporations to avoid *downsizing*, I want to create a work plan outline to be used to develop plans to improve businesses, invest in people, and stabilize the US economy. It is my belief that if senior managers use this template to organize meaningful plans for growth and success, *middle class* workers can benefit from higher wages and more stable work environments.

Important Points:

- *While Americans' average hourly pay has risen only six percent since 1985, German workers' pay has risen almost 30 percent.*[175]
- *The economy cannot possibly get out of its current doldrums without a strategy to revive the purchasing power of America's vast **middle class**. The spending of the richest five percent alone **will not lead** to a virtuous cycle of more jobs and higher living standards.*[176]
- A higher minimum wage would potentially reduce economic class inequality and allow those on the lower end of the spectrum an opportunity for economic mobility.
- It is important for corporations to utilize employee led groups that encourage ideas, participation, and creative thinking to help the company, and themselves secure their jobs.
- Strategic planning requires less time and less expense than most large scale *downsizing* strategies.
- It's critical to conduct research to determine specific trends in the marketplace that will benefit your business and avoid *downsizing*.
- Clearly defined leadership roles and infrastructure are the tools that ***implement*** a strategic plan.
- *Layoffs targeting just 1% of the workforce preceded, on average, a 31% increase in turnover.*[177]
- If any corporation compares the average cost of relocation to *downsizing*, they would break even or save money by investing resources to relocate an employee to another employer.
- *Counseling and training can help prepare employees for jobs with earnings comparable to their previous position.*[178]
- If the CEO or top tier pay exceeds a reasonable *proportion* then it should be reinvested for infrastructure, job training, or relocation services.

Needs Assessment:

These sample questions will help you obtain important information from your organization. You don't have to use all of them but you should ask at least 30 questions.

Participant Information: I recommend these surveys be anonymous but it can be helpful to know some demographic information about the respondent.

Age Group:

__ under 18 __ 18-25 __ 26-35 __ 36-55 __56-65 __ over 65

Profession:

__ student __ teacher __ manager __ worker

Education:

___ high school ___ college ___ graduate school

Tenure with organization:

_ 0 to 1 year _ 1 to 3 years _ 3 to 5 years __ more than 5 yrs

1) Describe the needs your organization fulfills.

2) Identify five revenue sources for your organization.

3) What are the concerns of the Board of Directors?

4) What are the concerns of Senior Management?

5) Describe our (core) programs, who we serve, and our intended outcomes?

6) What is my role in how to strengthen the organization?

7) What is the current climate in our market place and how is it affecting our organization?

8) I can see the connection between my work & contributions and our organization's success?

9) What three things motivate me?

10) Management is comfortable giving feedback and receiving feedback?

11) What is the most important priority for your organization to address over the next 12 months?

12) The management roles are clearly defined and respected?

13) The Board of Directors actively participates in an overall strategic planning process?

14) The Board members receive regular training?

15) Managers receive regular training?

16) Employees receive regular training?

17) Sufficient resources are allocated to ensure each program can achieve the established goals and objectives?

18) Staff has sufficient training, resources, and skill levels to produce the program?

19) Each program has performance indicators to ensure that the program meets its goals and objectives?

20) Every year, the organization evaluates its activities to determine progress toward goal accomplishment?

21) Periodically, the organization conducts a comprehensive evaluation of its programs. This evaluation measures program outcomes (impacts on clients or customers)?

22) The organization has systems in place to provide the appropriate information needed by staff and Board and Senior management to make sound financial decisions?

23) The organization's Board of Directors has established a committee (or task force) charged with developing, evaluating and reviewing policies, practices and goals?

24) List three ways that will advance the organization's cause or mission in the community?

25) Is the organization able to inspire people to join the cause and engage the community?

26) What is the Mission Statement for the organization?

27) If money were no object what initiative would you like to start to improve your organization and the people you serve?

28) List three things that concern you the most about this organization:

29) Who are the decision makers in your organization?

30) Does your organizations Website strategy fit with our corporate strategy?

31) How does your organization compare to the competition?

32) Describe your ideal customer.

33) What is your organizations main appeal to your target customer?

34) What needs and strategies do you need to improve support?

35) What do you observe that indicates there is a problem?

36) What types of things or measures would tell you that you are being successful?

37) What is happening in your business/department that shouldn't be happening?

38) What is happening in your business/department that should be happening?

39) What does excellent performance look like?

40) What does current performance look like?

41) What should these people be doing differently?

- ❏ Start: _____
- ❏ Stop: _____
- ❏ Continue: _____

42) What things other than knowledge and skills might be preventing employees from performing as they should?

43) What knowledge, skills, or behaviors do you think the employees need to learn to perform the way they should?

44) Work requirements, procedures, and goals are clearly understood for what is expected of you?

45) Do you receive consistent feedback against those expectations?

46) How do you know if the employees are doing well?

47) Are consequences aligned with expected performance, are there positive and negative consequences?

48) Does the technology support good work?

49) Is the needed information readily available?

50) Does the work environment support good ergonomics?

51) Are the people capable of learning and performing the job?

52) How familiar are the key partners and community members with the issues, products, or services you are trying to address?

53) What outreach efforts are made to educate the public about the issue, products, and the services you provide?

54) What additional products or services are needed in your community?

55) Is there collaboration between departments in your organization?

56) Are there any obstacles to accomplishing your mission?

57) If there are obstacles, how can they be resolved?

58) If you prefer someone to help you, whom do you usually ask?

59) Considering the features that you prefer in these systems/products or services, what makes them appealing to you?

60) What have you done when things went wrong?

61) What kinds of features do you think would attract new customers to use this system/product or service?

62) What other feedback would you like to give us on this needs assessment questionnaire?

Based on the needs assessment the following three areas represent opportunities that everyone can agree upon:

Based on these opportunities the following three goals will be attained in order to improve financial performance and maintain jobs:

Goal 1	Goal 2	Goal 3

The person(s) in charge of this transformation and goal attainment is:

Review process:

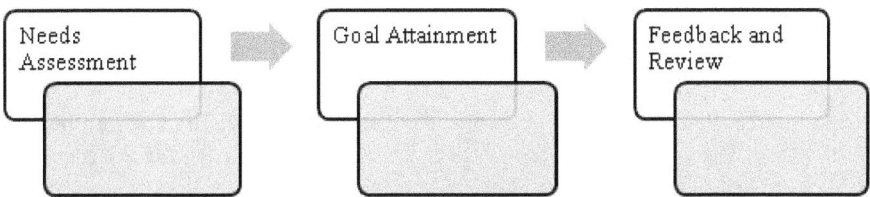

Needs Assessment → Goal Attainment → Feedback and Review

Dates for review:

❑ _____   ❑ _____

❑ _____   ❑ _____

❑ _____   ❑ _____

❑ _____   ❑ _____

Methods to avoid *downsizing* and improve financial performance while investing in the *middle class* and the US economy include:

- ❑ Include employee incentives for identification of cost savings
- ❑ Eliminate expense accounts or mileage payments
- ❑ Invest in employee health and wellness to increase performance and productivity.
- ❑ Creation of new workflows/teams.
- ❑ Lend or transfer employees to other companies using up-sizing.com or relocation services.
- ❑ Ask your customers and suppliers how to reduce costs and improve performance and productivity.
- ❑ Sell company assets to raise cash.
- ❑ Pay severance to American workers let go and train them for new jobs.
- ❑ Increase minimum wage to half of the median wage.
- ❑ Promote and/or fund higher education and training.
- ❑ Incentives for ideas that lead to innovation.
- ❑ Employee feedback groups.

❑ More Insourcing; less outsourcing.

Or:

_____

_____

Proportional Spending:

Use the following boxes to list the proportion of each expense category. Feel free to use dollar amounts as well as percentages. The idea is to keep these four financial metrics.

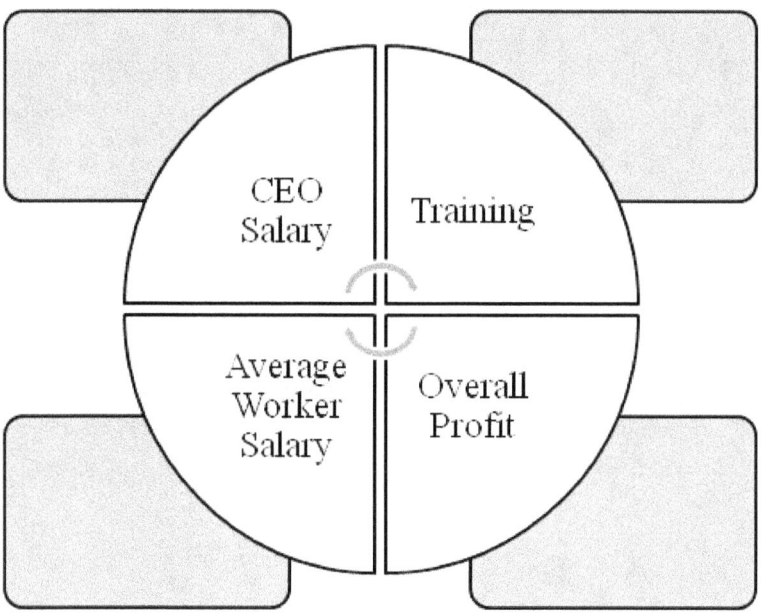

SUGGESTIONS & RESOURCES FOR PEOPLE AFFECTED BY *DOWNSIZING*

I spend a great deal of time in my community helping people find jobs. Trying to find a new job can be a grueling process that breaks confidence, shatters stability, and creates doubt and despair. I want to dedicate part of this book to helping people find new jobs. While the process can be taxing, I have proven methods that help people find jobs in any circumstance. One example is a friend of mine that was out of work for eight years. She was trained as a designer but spent her years consulting and teaching informally. The income generated from this venture was not enough to maintain her home and family life. After her savings expired she came to me for help. The first thing we did is re-tool her resume. This is the most difficult part of the process. While I outline the steps necessary to write an effective resume, it still remains difficult for people to find good in themselves when they're unemployed. By highlighting her accomplishments versus her job tasks she was able to successfully interview and obtain a full time teaching job with benefits. This provided new hope and momentum to bring her life more positive rewards and financial stability to help her family. I'm confident that if you follow the steps I've outlined below, you too will experience greater stability and positivity in your job search.

When *downsizing* becomes unavoidable and you and your family are affected by a real or suspected loss of your job it's important to have some key strategies to help your transition. Once again I use the power of three to provide you easy steps to be successful.

1. BE AWARE:

We don't always know when our companies may take a turn for the worse but there are typically warning signs. It is well known that it's better to look for a job when currently employed then when unemployed. So to help you get one step ahead of a possible job loss, look for these signs:

1. Consistent poor performance quarter after quarter.
2. Large shifts in stock prices.
3. Major leaders in the organization leave.
4. Companies leaving or moving locations.
5. Your market segment takes a hit or shows resistance.

Whether you see these signs or not, it's important to develop a strong strategy to realign yourself with new work and maintain stability in your home life and overall health.

When looking for a new job you may not be aware of what companies may be in the market for your specific skill set. I find it very useful to use Indeed.com and type in key words for searches. For example if you like training, use that as a key word. Other key words could include manager, planning, leadership, human resources, etc. What Indeed will do is send you any listing with those key words included. Indeed will also allow you to follow a specific company. Once you are done creating your searches Indeed will e-mail you daily new listings. At times displaced workers can't determine what they want to do next. This is a simple and easy way to explore companies, occupations, and other options.

I also recommend volunteering as a way to network and be noticed. Even though organizations reduce work force there is still a need for work, and as a result, there are more volunteer and internships available than ever before. What are the benefits of donating your time and working for free? 1) Gain job experience. 2) Network and meet people who may be able to hire you. 3) The company you volunteer for my end up hiring you.

Some organizations may not have a formal volunteer or internship program established. Help them develop one and convince them this relationship will benefit the organization and your ability to contribute to the community while looking for work. Internships are also an excellent way to prepare your children for their adult lives. Both Amanda and Justin participated in internships prior to going to college. This gave them real experience in their chosen field, professional work experience, and the ability to understand how their school career will transition to a professional career. The internship fit around their school and social schedule and provided them great value on their resume and college applications.

2. BUILDING YOUR RESUME:

The typical problem most people have on their resume is highlighting their accomplishments. The purpose of a resume is for someone to interview you. A human resources manager can look at over 100 applications a day. The first paragraph of an effective resume must stand out in the first 30 seconds of reading it. How can you accomplish this? 1) Your objective must be specific to the job *and* company. What does that mean? That means your objective must match the mission statement or goals of the company to which you are applying. This information can be found easily on their website or searching Google for related articles. Try to talk to people already doing the job for which you're applying. Talking to people can provide insight for use later in the process. Next, make sure you write with your heart and be sincere. When you write your objectives and accomplishments you must be specific. If you're applying for a human resources job highlight accomplishments relating to people, training, and coaching. This means if you're applying for 10 different positions, you should have 10 different specific resumes.

Many people list experiences in their resume. A secretary can write *answers phones, files, can work with Office 2010*. A better approach is to list accomplishments of your last position such as "employee of the month" or "received largest increase of our group". Typically, the last portion of your resume includes your education and community involvement. These two aspects of your resume show your stability and experience. A strong resume should not be more than one page.

Once you submit your resume it may be necessary to follow up on the process. Some companies handle phone calls and follow up on applications differently. Stay professional and patient when following up on your status.

If your resume is built successfully mirroring the company's objectives and highlighting your accomplishments in a clear and concise manner, the next step is the interview. Instead of memorizing types of questions that can be answered, take time to understand what the company is looking for by learning about their mission, current financial trends, and current projects. Always prepare a question to ask your interviewer. One good type of question is a futuristic question such as "how do you see your company/industry changing in the next five years?" Before leaving the interview, always restate what your purpose is and why this interview/job is important to you and your family. In addition you must **ask for the job.** The basic principle of selling is *you don't get what you don't ask for.* Companies want honest, hard working people to help them achieve their goals. Your job in the interview is to ensure them that you're that person.

Here is a format for an effective resume:

Your Name
Address
Contact Phone
E-mail

Objective:
(one sentence tied to your passion for working in this environment) (one sentence tied to the organization's mission and values as listed on their website). You must tie your experience and passions to those of the company.

If this objective does not capture the attention and interest of the HR manager in the first 30 seconds, you will not get an interview.

Work Experience:
This must include accomplishments under your title and length of employment. Some accomplishments you can include:

Suggestions and Resources

1. Received two raises in one year.
2. Responsible for training new employees.
3. Employee of the month
4. Received an award for most productive
5. Received excellent review ratings three years in a row
6. Have only missed one day of work in three years

Education:
This can include any training or formal education after high school. If you are reading a book or taking a course to improve yourself, it should be listed here.

Community:
It's important to list personal interests and community involvement in this section. The hiring manager wants a

well-rounded person and this section is important to your overall candidacy.

Here's what a sample looks like if you were looking to join Boeing. Notice how the objective is specific to the company and or the job you are looking for. Also notice how the accomplishments are listed.

Recommendations:
Include two letters of recommendations with your resume. This will help give you a competitive advantage.

Your Name

Address
City, State and Zip
Phone: Email: Website:

Career Objective: To use my passion for helping people and my heightened work ethic to contribute to a company committed to excellence in both design and service. My depth and experience in developing others should be matched by the company I join. Boeing's values of leadership skills training, high ethical standards, total customer satisfaction, encourage cooperative efforts, and promote the health and well-being of our total community is in line with my own values and ethical compass.

Career Accomplishments:

Your Company 2005 to Present: City and State
- Promoted three times in the last five years.
- Employee of the month each year for the last seven years
- Successfully manage a team that exceeded productivity expectations.
- Successful in driving customer satisfaction

Your Company 2000 to 2005: City and State
- Deemed most productive in word processing
- Perfect attendance award
- Designated as a trainer for other employees.

Education:

- Any degree or certification
- Training or classes taken at previous employment
- What you've done outside of work to learn; e.g. seminars or books

Community Involvement:

- Parent Volunteer
- Performed community service for habitat for humanity, humane society, and the American Cancer Society.
- Assist women who have been victim of abuse or neglect.

References upon request.

3. CONTINUED EDUCATION:

As mentioned earlier in the book training is extremely valuable to helping you find a new job or develop new skills. While you're employed take advantage of as much training as you can. Typically the training companies provide is at no charge. If you seek specialized training invest a small amount into trade schools, community colleges, professional seminars, or recommended books as a way to increase your knowledge and expand your employment opportunities. The US Department of Labor offers training options on their site at http://www.dol.gov/dol/topic/training/ . Those who are employed, underemployed, or unemployed should take advantage of these resources. Goodwill Industries is another great source for people needing training and job placement. In 2012 Goodwill Industries provided employment and training programs to 6.7 million people in the US. [179] There are also national service programs like AmeriCorps, the Peace Corps, and Teach for America that provide free on-the-job training, a job, and an education award that can be applied to future college classes.[180]

Training can also include reading books, going to seminars, or joining a Union. While it may be difficult to find time and resources to engage in additional learning opportunities it is a critical step to take. The best and fastest way to increase your wage is to increase your skills.

From the first page of this book I wanted the reader to understand my willingness to help people throughout the US as it relates to *downsizing*. We've gone through the history of *downsizing* and how it affects our economy through consumer spending, job loss versus unemployment, and economic class inequality. We also tried to understand Wall Street's role in shaping the way companies analyze and allocate growing profits. Some of the investments we explored were corporate social responsibilities. Through exploring the proven research of diminished financial performance from companies that have *downsized*, we explored financial reasons for companies to reinvest their profits into people.

Through training and relocation, companies would maintain their current profit levels by cutting costs associated with *downsizing*. By using expert advice on how to avoid *downsizing*, companies could improve their business by involving a thoughtful strategic planning process and involving employees in the decision making process of those plans.

We read about companies like Costco, GE, GM, KEEN, and others who are adding more jobs and investing in their people which has brought them financial success. With their contributions and other companies following suit, we can grow the US economy and consumer spending by strengthening the *middle class* through *insourcing* and a national job exchange program (up-sizing.com). While these are just a few examples of what adding jobs could look like, this book has proven that corporate profits can only be strengthened when invested in their people.

While these ideas and principles are easy to understand, they are not easily adaptable to our established Wall Street rules. CEOs are rewarded for following the rules not redefining them. In some small way I hope this book helps Wall Street experts and top CEOs realize they are the true leaders responsible for strengthening our US economy. If you are not investing a small portion of wealth to strengthen the *middle class*, then, as we've seen in this book, you are weakening more than a nation, but your company as well.

If you have experienced **downsizing** like I have, I hope you are walking away with a better understanding of how to help yourself, your family, and your company avoid any financial instability. Take advantage of getting involved at work and investing in more education. While I know being eliminated from work is degrading and difficult to cope with, it is important that you follow the resume format and job search recommendations so you can quickly repair your situation and regain respect and financial stability.

Giving back and helping people does not sound much like a financial plan. But if you read closely, there is plenty of research to suggest that being socially responsible with corporate profits produces greater financial results over time. These facts and recent statistics are hard to ignore, change never comes easy. Charles Darwin once wrote: *It is not the strongest of the species that survives, nor the most intelligent that survives.* **It is the one that is the most adaptable to change**. Consumer spending, inequality in economic class, and extreme job loss in our US economy cannot be ignored. All corporations must adapt to what we know so we can build a better future for your company, your town, and your country.

[1] Macy's Marches Down A New Path by Lisa LaMotta. Forbes Magazine; February 2nd, 2009.

[2] Macy's Marches Down A New Path by Lisa LaMotta. Forbes Magazine; February 2nd, 2009.

[3] $8-Billion Loss Posted by IBM; More Layoffs Set by SCOT J. PALTROW and JONATHAN WEBER. July 28, 1993.

[4] $8-Billion Loss Posted by IBM; More Layoffs Set by SCOT J. PALTROW and JONATHAN WEBER. July 28, 1993.

[5] THE DOWNSIZING OF AMERICA; Big Holes Where the Dignity Used to Be
By RICK BRAGG Published: March 05, 1996. New York Times.
http://www.nytimes.com/1996/03/05/us/the-downsizing-of-america-big-holes-where-the-dignity-used-to-be.html?pagewanted=all&src=pm
.

[6] Cameron, Kim S.(1994).Strategies for Successful Organizational Downsizing. Human
Resource Management,33,(2),189(23).

[7] Reducing Slack: The performance consequences of downsizing by large industridal firms, 1977-93, Strategic Management Journal Strat. Mgmt. J., 26: 1087–1108 (2005)

[8] Nohria, Dyer, and Dalzell, 2002

[9] THE EFFECTS OF DOWNSIZING ON SURVIVORS: A META-ANALYSIS
GLADYS B. WEST James F. Wolf, Chair, et al. MAY 12, 2000.

[10] Cameron, K. S. (1994), Strategies for Successful Organizational Downsizing, Human Resource Management, 33(2): 189-211.

[11] US suffers largest job loss since February 1991 By David Walsh, 5 May 2001.

[12] US suffers largest job loss since February 1991 By David Walsh, 5 May 2001.

[13] http://stats.oecd.org/glossary/detail.asp?ID=3556

[14] http://www.investopedia.com/terms/u/unemployment.asp

[15] Farber HS. "What Do We Know About Job Loss in the U.S.? Evidence From the Displaced Workers Survey, 1984–2004" Economic Perspectives. 2005;2Q:13–28.

[16] Don't Blame Trade For U.S. Job Losses Excerpted from The McKinsey Quarterly; Forbes November 10, 2005.
http://www.forbes.com/2005/11/10/trade-jobs-economy-cx_1110mckinsey.html

[17] Bureau of Labor Statistics (2010). "Worker Displacement: 2007-2009." News Release. USDL- 10-1174. Available at www.bls.gov/news.release/disp.nr0.htm.

[18] Unemployment and Earnings Losses: The Long-Term Impacts of The Great Recession on American Workers, Released: November 2011, by Adam Looney • Policy Director, The Hamilton Project; Senior Fellow, The Brookings Institution and Michael Greenstone • Director, The Hamilton Project; 3M Professor of Environmental Economics, MIT; Senior Fellow, The Brookings Institution.

[19] The Great Jobs Recession Goes On; The recession is officially over but unemployment remains high By Mortimer B. Zuckerman, US News, February 11, 2011.

[20] Consumer spending: an engine for U.S. job growth by Mitra Toossi. Monthly Labor Review November 2002.

[21] http://www.infoplease.com/ipa/A0104719.html

[22] Consumer spending: an engine for U.S. job growth by Mitra Toossi. Monthly Labor Review November 2002.

[23] Spending our way to disaster; The consumer debt bubble in the United States could make the stock bubble seem like nothing. October 3, 2003:By Justin Lahart, CNN/Money Senior Writer. http://money.cnn.com/2003/10/02/markets/consumerbubble/

[24] http://www.census.gov/retail/

[25] http://www.nrf.com/modules.php?name=Pages&sp_id=1140

[26] http://www.data360.org/dsg.aspx?Data_Set_G roup_Id=2035&page=3&count=100

[27] http://www.infoplease.com/ipa/A0104719.html

[28]
http://www.data360.org/dsg.aspx?Data_Set_Group_Id=2035&page=2 &count=100

[29]
http://www.data360.org/dsg.aspx?Data_Set_Group_Id=2035&page=2 &count=100

[30] An Economy That Works; Job Creation and America's Future by James Manyika, Susan Lund, et al. June 2011.

[31] An Economy That Works; Job Creation and America's Future by James Manyika, Susan Lund, et al. June 2011. Pg. 1

[32] http://www.infoplease.com/ipa/A0104719.html

[33] Fed: Consumer Spending Down $7,300 Per Person Since Great Recession Began By Carla Fried; Money Watch/ July 12, 2011.

[34] http://en.wikipedia.org/wiki/Charging_Bull

[35] http://www.incademy.com/courses/Bear-market-investing/How-to-spot-the-appearance-of-a-bear-market/4/1015/10002

[36] Stocks boosted by strong profit reports from Wall Street banks; Investors see the bank earnings reports as another sign that the economy is improving. By Andrew Tangel. July 19, 2013

[37] http://www.cbsnews.com/8301-505123_162-57598652/stocks-dive-on-fed-fears-weaker-corporate-profits/

[38] Recovery in U.S. Is Lifting Profits, but Not Adding Jobs by Nelson D. Schwartz. Published: March 3, 2013.
[39] Wealth, Income, and Power by G. William Domhoff.
[40] Wolff, E. N. (2012). The Asset Price Meltdown and the Wealth of the Middle Class. New York: New York University.
[41] Wealth, Income, and Power by G. William Domhoff.
[42] It's the Inequality, Stupid by Dave Gilson and Carolyn Perot. March/April 2011 Issue.
[43] It's the Inequality, Stupid by Dave Gilson and Carolyn Perot. March/April 2011 Issue.
[44] Did the 'Lost' Middle Class Become Upper Class? By Robert Frank on Wednesday, August 22, 2012.
[45] Did the 'Lost' Middle Class Become Upper Class? By Robert Frank on Wednesday, August 22, 2012.
[46]
http://www.alternet.org/story/145705/the_richest_1_have_captured_america%27s_wealth_--_what%27s_it_going_to_take_to_get_it_back
[47] How the Middle Class Is Shrinking By Rick Newman. October 15, 2010.
[48] http://www.cbo.gov/about/overview
[49] Income Gaps Between Very Rich and Everyone Else More Than Tripled In Last Three Decades, By Arloc Sherman and Chad Stone. June 25, 2010. Figures throughout this paper were adjusted by CBO for inflation and are presented in 2007 dollars.
[50] Income Gaps Between Very Rich and Everyone Else More Than Tripled In Last Three Decades, By Arloc Sherman and Chad Stone. June 25, 2010.
[51] Obama Focuses on Economy, Vowing to Help Middle Class by Michael D. Shear and Peter Baker. Published: July 24, 2013.
[52] The truth about 'class war' in America by Richard Wolff. September 19, 2011.
[53] The truth about 'class war' in America by Richard Wolff. September 19, 2011.
[54] Why Inequality is the Real Cause of Our Ongoing Terrible Economy by Robert Reich. September 4, 2011.
[55] http://devoutinfidel.wordpress.com/2011/09/30/occupy-wall-st-releases-their-mission-statement/
[56] The United States of... Class War, Inequality, and Poverty by Jon Queally. July 28, 2013 by Common Dreams.
[57] The United States of... Class War, Inequality, and Poverty by Jon Queally. July 28, 2013 by Common Dreams.
[58] http://bigstory.ap.org/article/exclusive-4-5-us-face-near-poverty-no-work-0
[59] MIDDLE CLASS IN AMERICA Prepared by the U. S. Department Of Commerce Economics and Statistics Administration for the Office

of the Vice President of the nited States Middle Class Task Force. January 2010.

[60] MIDDLE CLASS IN AMERICA Prepared by the U. S. Department Of Commerce Economics and Statistics Administration for the Office of the Vice President of the nited States Middle Class Task Force. January 2010. Page 24.

[61] The Effect of Health Care Cost Growth on the U.S. Economy Final Report for Task Order # HP-06-12. Prepared for the Office of the Assistant Secretary for Planning and Evaluation, United States Department of Health and Human Services.

[62] http://www.justfacts.com/healthcare.asp Calculated with data from: a) Dataset: "National Health Expenditures by Type of Service and Source of Funds, Calendar Years 1960-2009." U.S. Department of Health & Human Services, Centers for Medicare and Medicaid Services, January 5, 2011. https://www.cms.gov/, b) Dataset: "Consumer Price Index, All Urban Consumers (CPI-U), U.S. City Average, All items." U.S. Department of Labor, Bureau of Labor Statistics, September 15, 2011.
ftp://ftp.bls.gov/pub/special.requests/cpi/cpiai.txt and
c) Table 1.1.5: "Gross Domestic Product." United States Department of Commerce, Bureau of Economic Analysis. Last revised August 26, 2011. http://www.bea.gov/.

[64] http://www.justfacts.com/healthcare.asp#[1]

[65] Where 'Class Warfare' Really Comes From By Susan Milligan. April 9, 2012.

[66] The Case Against Corporate Social Responsibility By Aneel Karnani. August 23, 2010.

[67] Is corporate social responsibility profitable for companies? By Floyd Whaley on February 20, 2013.

[68] Is corporate social responsibility profitable for companies? By Floyd Whaley on February 20, 2013.

[69] Is corporate social responsibility profitable for companies? By Floyd Whaley on February 20, 2013.

[70] http://data.worldbank.org/indicator/CM.MKT.LCAP.CD

[71] http://www.bea.gov/newsreleases/national/pi/pinewsrelease.htm

[72] http://www.huffingtonpost.com/2013/09/13/uneven-financial-crisis-recovery-charts_n_3913882.html

[73] Spending our way to disaster; The consumer debt bubble in the United States could make the stock bubble seem like nothing. October 3, 2003:By Justin Lahart, CNN/Money Senior Writer.
http://money.cnn.com/2003/10/02/markets/consumerbubble/

[74] Recovery in U.S. Is Lifting Profits, but Not Adding Jobs by Nelson D. Schwartz. Published: March 3, 2013.

[75] Did the 'Lost' Middle Class Become Upper Class? By Robert Frank

on Wednesday, August 22, 2012.

[76] Did the 'Lost' Middle Class Become Upper Class? By Robert Frank on Wednesday, August 22, 2012.

[77] How do Shareholders respond to layoff announcements? A meta-analysis by Gunther Capelle-Blacard. Université Paris 1 Panthéon-Sorbonne, Nicolas COUDERC, ESCP-EAP, July 2008.

[78] Worrell, D. L., Davidson, W. N. and Sharma, V.M. (1991), Layoff Announcements and Stockholder Wealth, Academy of Management Journal, 34: 662-678.

[79] De Meuse, K. P., Vanderheiden, P. A. and Bergmann, T. J. (1994), Announced Layoffs: Their Effect on Corporate Financial Performance, Human Resource Management, 33(4): 509-530.

[80] Cascio, W. F., Young, C. and Morris, J. (1997), Financial Consequences of Employment Change Decisions in Major US Corporations, Academy of Management Journal, 40(5): 1175-1189.

[81] Morris, J. R., Cascio W. F. and Young, C. E. (1999), Downsizing After All These Years: Questions and Answers about Who Did It, How Many Did It, and Who Benefited from It. Organizational Dynamics, Winter 1999: 78-87.

[82] New evidence regarding organizational downsizing and a firm's financial performance: a long-term analysis by De Meuse, Kenneth P., Bergmann, Thomas J., et al. Pub Date: 06/22/2004; Journal of Managerial Issues Publisher: Pittsburg State University - Department of Economics Audience: Date: Summer, 2004 Source Volume: 16 Source Issue: 2.

[83] http://investor.cisco.com/stocklookup.cfm?NavSection=StockInfo&historic_Month=8&historic_Day=20&historic_Year=2000

[84] http://www.forbes.com/2000/01/20/feat.html

[85] http://www.nasdaq.com/symbol/bby/pe-ratio

[86] http://finance.yahoo.com/q/hp?s=BBY&a=05&b=1&c=2000&d=11&e=1&f=2000&g=d

[87] http://www.gurufocus.com/term/pettm/BBY/P%252FE%2BRatio%2528ttm%2529/Best%2BBuy%2BCo%2BInc

[88] http://www.nasdaq.com/symbol/hbc/analyst-research

[89] http://www.nasdaq.com/symbol/hbc/pe-ratio

[90] http://investing.money.msn.com/investments/charts?symbol=HBC#{%22zRange%22:%229%22,%22startDate%22:%222003-8-21%22,%22endDate%22:%222013-8-21%22,%22chartStyle%22:%22mountain%22,%22chartCursor%22:%221%22,%22scaleType%22:%220%22,%22yaxisAlign%22:%22right%22,%22mode%22:%22pan%22}

[91] http://finance.yahoo.com/q?s=GE

[92] http://abcnews.go.com/Business/story?id=3461720&page=1

[93] An Analysis on Best Buy's Customer-Centric Innovation by Hoang Nguyen, November 14th, 2010.

[94] Costco CEO Craig Jelinek Leads the Cheapest, Happiest Company in the World
By Brad Stone; June 06, 2013. Bloomberg Business Week.

[95] Costco CEO Craig Jelinek Leads the Cheapest, Happiest Company in the World
By Brad Stone; June 06, 2013. Bloomberg Business Week.

[96] Costco CEO Craig Jelinek Leads the Cheapest, Happiest Company in the World
By Brad Stone; June 06, 2013. Bloomberg Business Week.

[97] U.S. Retail Industry CEO Five-Year Compensation Comparison Chart 2004 - 2009
Complete Salary and Bonus Package Figures For Top Retail Industry Executives By Barbara Farfan.
http://retailindustry.about.com/od/topusretailcompanies/a/us-Retail-CEO-Total-Compensation-2005-2007-2007-2009-2009-Top-Retail-Industry-Salary.htm

[98] Jim Sinegal: Costco CEO Focuses on Employees Sinegal is one of America's Best Leaders because he's not a typical CEO By Amanda Ruggeri; October 22, 2009.

[99] http://www.smartbrief.com/02/04/09/costco-ceo-sees-no-need-layoffs#.UiXig3-abYg

[100] The State of Retail Workforce Management Benchmark Study: November 2007 By: Nikki Baird.

[101] Few Retailers Implement Customer Centric Approaches, Says Study; Nov 7, 2007 http://voices.yahoo.com/few-retailers-implement-customer-centric-approaches-645568.html

[102] Employment Downsizing and its Alternatives; Strategies for Long-Term Success by Wayne F. Cascio. ©2009 SHRM Foundation.

[103] http://www.ips-dc.org/reports/executive_excess_2010 . Executive Excess 2010: CEO Pay and the Great Recession By Sarah Anderson, Chuck Collins, Sam Pizzigati, Kevin Shih.

[104] http://www.dailyfinance.com/2011/09/15/layoffs-leave-everyone-worse-off/ . Layoffs Leave Everyone Worse Off by Frank Koller Sep 15th 2011.

[105] 17th Annual Executive Compensation Survey by By Sarah Anderson, Chuck Collins,
Sam Pizzigati, and Kevin Shih, September 1, 2010.

[106] Mass Layoffs Plump CEO Pockets By Ann Binlot; CNET/ September 1, 2010.

[107] Mass Layoffs Plump CEO Pockets By Ann Binlot; CNET/ September 1, 2010.

[108] CEO's lay off thousands; rake in Millions by Roland Jones; NBC News September 1st, 2010.

[109] The 10 Highest-Paid CEOs Who Laid Off The Most Workers: Institute For Policy Studies; Huffington Post, by Nathaniel Cahners Hindman, 09/01/10.

[110] The 10 Highest-Paid CEOs Who Laid Off The Most Workers: Institute For Policy Studies; Huffington Post, by Nathaniel Cahners Hindman, 09/01/10.

[111] 10 CEOs Who Got Rich By Squeezing Workers by Josh Harkinson; Mother Jones, Thu May. 12, 2011.

[112] The Clinton Presidency: http://clinton5.nara.gov/WH/Accomplishments/eightyears-03.html

[113] The Clinton Presidency: http://clinton5.nara.gov/WH/Accomplishments/eightyears-03.html

[114] The Clinton Presidency: http://clinton5.nara.gov/WH/Accomplishments/eightyears-03.html

[115] A shrinking middle class means a shrinking economy, By Alan Krueger
January 13, 2012.

[116] Unemployment and Earnings Losses: The Long-Term Impacts of The Great Recession on American Workers, Released: November 2011, by Adam Looney, Policy Director, The Hamilton Project; Senior Fellow, The Brookings Institution and Michael Greenstone, Director, The Hamilton Project; 3M Professor of Environmental Economics, MIT; Senior Fellow, The Brookings Institution.

[117] Unemployment and Earnings Losses: The Long-Term Impacts of The Great Recession on American Workers, Released: November 2011, by Adam Looney, Policy Director, The Hamilton Project; Senior Fellow, The Brookings Institution and Michael Greenstone, Director, The Hamilton Project; 3M Professor of Environmental Economics, MIT; Senior Fellow, The Brookings Institution.

[118] An Economy That Works; Job Creation and America's Future by James Manyika, Susan Lund, et al. June 2011.

[119] The annual report of the council of economic advisers by Alan B. Krueger
Chairman, Washington, D.C., March 15, 2013.

[120] Factors underlying the effect of organisational downsizing on health of employees: longitudinal cohort study by Mika Kivimäki, Jussi Vahtera, Jaana Pentti, Jane E Ferrie. BMJ Volume 320, April 8th, 2000.

[121] Organisational Restructuring/Downsizing, OHS Regulation and Worker Health and Wellbeing by Michael Quinlan, School of Organisation and Management, University of New South Wales, Sydney, Australia; March 2007.

[122] Bohle, P., Quinlan, M. & Mayhew, C., (2001), 'The health effects of job insecurity: An evaluation of the evidence', Economic and Labour

Relations Review, 12(1): 32-60.

[123] Strazdins, L., D'Souza, R., Lim, L., Broom, D. & Rodgers, B. (2004), 'Job strain, job insecurity, and health: Rethinking the relationship' Journal of Occupational Health Psychology, 9(4): 296-305.

[124] Organisational Restructuring/Downsizing, OHS Regulation and Worker Health and Wellbeing by Michael Quinlan, School of Organisation and Management, University of New South Wales, Sydney, Australia; March 2007.

[125] Greenglass, E., Burke, R. J., & Moore, K. A. (2003). Reactions to increased workload: Effects on professional efficacy of nurses. Applied Psychology: An International Review, 52(4), 580-597.

[126] How do Shareholders respond to layoff announcements? A meta-analysis by Gunther Capelle-Blacard. Université Paris 1 Panthéon-Sorbonne, Nicolas COUDERC, ESCP-EAP, July 2008.

[127] De Meuse, K. P., Vanderheiden, P. A. and Bergmann, T. J. (1994), Announced Layoffs: Their Effect on Corporate Financial Performance, Human Resource Management, 33(4): 509-530.

[128] Employment Downsizing and its Alternatives; Strategies for Long-Term Success by Wayne F. Cascio. ©2009 SHRM Foundation.

[129] http://www.ips-dc.org/reports/executive_excess_2010 . Executive Excess 2010: CEO Pay and the Great Recession By Sarah Anderson, Chuck Collins, Sam Pizzigati, Kevin Shih.

[130] An Economy That Works; Job Creation and America's Future by James Manyika, Susan Lund, et al. June 2011.

[131] Alternatives to Downsizing: An Organizational Innovation Approach by William Marty Martin, Audrey C. Davis. International Journal of Business and Social Research (IJBSR), Volume -3, No.-7, July, 2013

[132] Alternatives to Downsizing: An Organizational Innovation Approach by William Marty Martin, Audrey C. Davis. International Journal of Business and Social Research (IJBSR), Volume -3, No.-7, July, 2013

[133] Insourcing at GE: The Real Story by Brad Power. Harvard Business Review July 15, 2013.

[134] Why Inequality is the Real Cause of Our Ongoing Terrible Economy by Robert Reich. September 4, 2011.

[135] Why Inequality is the Real Cause of Our Ongoing Terrible Economy by Robert Reich. September 4, 2011.

[136] Why Inequality is the Real Cause of Our Ongoing Terrible Economy by Robert Reich. September 4, 2011.

[137] Can the Middle Class Be Saved? By Don Peck Jul 24 2011.

[138] Can the Middle Class Be Saved? By Don Peck Jul 24 2011.

[139] Insourcing at GE: The Real Story by Brad Power. Harvard Business Review July 15, 2013.

[140] Insourcing at GE: The Real Story by Brad Power. Harvard Business Review July 15, 2013.

[141] GM Bets on Insourcing, Brings Back 10,000 IT Jobs By Stephanie Overby; Fri, October 05, 2012.

[142] GM Bets on Insourcing, Brings Back 10,000 IT Jobs By Stephanie Overby; Fri, October 05, 2012.

[143] http://www.whitehouse.gov/blog/2012/01/11/everything-you-need-know-about-insourcing

[144] http://www.whitehouse.gov/blog/2012/01/11/everything-you-need-know-about-insourcing

[145] http://www.whitehouse.gov/blog/2012/01/11/everything-you-need-know-about-insourcing

[146] http://www.nasdaq.com/article/insourcing-a-silver-lining-ahead-analyst-blog-cm252697

[147] Unions Make The Middle Class by David Madland, Karla Walter, and Nick Burner. April 2011.

[148] Unions Make The Middle Class by David Madland, Karla Walter, and Nick Burner. April 2011. Page Three.

[149] Unions Make The Middle Class by David Madland, Karla Walter, and Nick Burner. April 2011. Page Five.

[150] The Union of the Sates; Center for Economic Policy Research. By John Scmitt, 2010.

[151]

http://www.americanprogressaction.org/issues/labor/report/2012/01/25/10913/unions-make-democracy-work-for-the-middle-class/

[152] Unions, Norms, and the Rise in U.S. Wage Inequality by Bruce Westerna and Jake Rosenfeld. August 2013.

[153] What have unions done for us? By Donna Brazile, CNN Contributor, September 4, 2012.

[154]What have unions done for us? By Donna Brazile, CNN Contributor, September 4, 2012.

[155] Why Screwing Unions Screws the Entire Middle Class Plus: How much income have you given up for the top 1 percent? By Kevin Drum. March/April 2011 Issue Mother Jones.

[156] Reducing Slack: The performance consequences of downsizing by large industridal firms, 1977-93, Strategic Management Journal Strat. Mgmt. J., 26: 1105 (2005)

[157] http://www.businessdictionary.com/definition/strategic-planning.html

[158] http://www.forbes.com/sites/aileron/2011/10/25/five-steps-to-a-strategic-plan/

[159] http://www.forbes.com/sites/aileron/2011/10/25/five-steps-to-a-strategic-plan/

[160] http://www.forbes.com/sites/aileron/2011/10/25/five-steps-to-a-strategic-plan/

[161] http://oas.samhsa.gov/NSDUH/2k9NSDUH/2k9ResultsP.pdf , page 73.

[162] http://oas.samhsa.gov/NSDUH/2k9NSDUH/2k9ResultsP.pdf , page 81.

[163] http://www.city-data.com/city/Vancouver-Washington.html

[164] AP Economic Stress Index, Clark County WA, 2010, http://hosted.ap.org/specials/interactives/_national/stress_index/

[165] The Cost of Downsizing By Todd A. Samuelson, CPA, Partner, June 10, 2009. http://www.umbaugh.com/the-cost-of-downsizing

[166] http://www.paragonrelocation.com/blog/index.php/corporate-relocation-cost/

[167] Halting the Exodus After a Layoff; Harvard Business Review, May 2008.

[168] How much does it cost companies to lose employees? By Suzanne Lucas, Money Watch; November 21, 2012. http://www.cbsnews.com/8301-505125_162-57552899/how-much-does-it-cost-companies-to-lose-employees/

[169] How much does it cost companies to lose employees? By Suzanne Lucas, Money Watch; November 21, 2012. http://www.cbsnews.com/8301-505125_162-57552899/how-much-does-it-cost-companies-to-lose-employees/

[170] U.S. Census Bureau, "County Business Patterns," July 2010, <http://www.census.gov/econ/cbp/index.html>.

[171] U.S. Census Bureau, "County Business Patterns," July 2010, <http://www.census.gov/econ/cbp/index.html>.

[172] Alternatives to Downsizing: An Organizational Innovation Approach by William Marty Martin, Audrey C. Davis. International Journal of Business and Social Research (IJBSR), Volume -3, No.-7, July, 2013

[173] Unemployment and Earnings Losses: The Long-Term Impacts of The Great Recession on American Workers, Released: November 2011, by Adam Looney, Policy Director, The Hamilton Project; Senior Fellow, The Brookings Institution and Michael Greenstone, Director, The Hamilton Project; 3M Professor of Environmental Economics, MIT; Senior Fellow, The Brookings Institution.

[174] http://www.dailyfinance.com/2011/09/15/layoffs-leave-everyone-worse-off/ . Layoffs Leave Everyone Worse Off by Frank Koller Sep 15th 2011.

[175] Why Inequality is the Real Cause of Our Ongoing Terrible Economy by Robert Reich. September 4, 2011.

[176] Why Inequality is the Real Cause of Our Ongoing Terrible Economy by Robert Reich. September 4, 2011.

[177] Halting the Exodus After a Layoff; Harvard Business Review, May 2008.

[178] Unemployment and Earnings Losses: The Long-Term Impacts of

The Great Recession on American Workers, Released: November 2011, by Adam Looney, Policy Director, The Hamilton Project; Senior Fellow, The Brookings Institution and Michael Greenstone, Director, The Hamilton Project; 3M Professor of Environmental Economics, MIT; Senior Fellow, The Brookings Institution.
[179] http://www.goodwill.org/about-us/our-mission/#
[180] 5 ways to get free job training by Christina Couch. Aug. 5, 2009.

ABOUT THE AUTHOR:

Brad Lebowsky has been in management roles for more than 25 years. Brad has combined his 30-year track record of excellence in retail store management and corporate training, with 19 years of carrying out successful fundraising, strategic planning, and leadership training for a variety of non-profit organizations.

Brad devotes his energy to organizations that are committed to success and growth. Using his education, experience, and ability to lead teams, Brad adds value to his team and his organization, while helping to maintain work -life blend as the ultimate reward for energy and hard work.

For inquiries please contact Brad via his website: www.BradLebowsky.com or e-mail Brad at: upsizing@comcast.net

ISBN-13: 9781492763642
ISBN-10: 1492763640

The majority of profits from this book endeavor will be directly invested in developing www.up-sizing.com to facilitate job exchanges throughout the United States.